THE RHYTHM BOOK

BEGINNING NOTATION AND SIGHT-READING

By Rory Stuart

To access audio visit:
www.halleonard.com/mylibrary

Enter Code
3238-5155-7209-7425

Design and layout by Matthew Heister

ISBN 978-1-5400-1257-9

7777 W. BLUEMOUND RD. P.O. BOX 13819 MILWAUKEE, WI 53213

In Australia Contact:
Hal Leonard Australia Pty. Ltd.
4 Lentara Court
Cheltenham, Victoria, 3192 Australia
Email: ausadmin@halleonard.com.au

Visit Hal Leonard Online at
www.halleonard.com

"Rory's vast knowledge and long experience in teaching rhythm makes his material essential for any musician interested in developing their rhythmic ability!"

- ANDERS VESTERGÅRD
(Swedish percussionist and rhythm professor at Fridhems Flkhögskola)

"Professor Rory Stuart has been an inspiration for generations of jazz musicians for decades. His rhythmic approach is innovative and engaging, and his playing and composition skills are second to none. This is a fundamental book for every jazz musician"

- DR. RICARDO PINHEIRO
(Professor at Universidade Lusíada de Lisboa, Portugal)

"As a fellow teacher who has studied rhythm with Rory, I can say he truly is a teacher's teacher. His precise and innovative instruction lifts my level of creativity and skill. His thorough coverage of rhythmic options allows for a massive expansion of concept, but he does it with an organizational structure in which it feels simple to learn and grow. Rory's method is genius and has taken so many young people to a new level that he has influenced a whole generation of jazz!"

- RACHEL Z
(Pianist, USA)

"Rhythm is a broad, complex and fascinating world to study and try to describe in a clear and compelling way. In his different volumes, Rory succeeds in giving the reader a great variety of examples and theories drawn from the most simple foundation to the most advanced concepts. I was lucky to collaborate with Rory, both as a student and performer, and was always inspired by his continuous search for higher rhythmic mastery. I can only encourage every musician, regardless of their level of understanding, to study using Rory's great writings.

- ARTHUR HNATEK
(Drummer from Switzerland)

"The depth of Rory Stuart's rhythmic teaching is as inspiring as it is humbling. By far, one of the clearest, most refreshing masters of this knowledge..."

- DANIEL DOR
(Drummer from Israel)

"Before coming to NYC and meeting up with Rory Stuart I really had no idea how fascinating the world of rhythm was. Rory was like an open door to so many worlds of music, both in the sense of style and approaches of rhythm. Some things I take from his classes will always be a part of my music."

- ARI BRAGI KARASON
(Trumpeter from Iceland)

"During my four years at the New School, Rory Stuart was one of the kindest, most supportive and inspiring teachers I had the pleasure of studying with. His approach to rhythm influenced my music so deeply that I still find myself drawing from that inspiration when I write, not to mention, of all the music I wrote those four years. My best tunes came out of Rory's classes!"

- BECCA STEVENS
(Vocalist and Composer, USA)

Errata Sheet

Eighth Note Exercises with Pickups

Here are some exercises with pickups:

Exercise 1-084:

Exercise 1-085:

Exercise 1-086:

Exercise 1-087:

Exercise 1-088:

Exercise 1-089:

Exercise 1-090:

Exercise 1-091:

Eighth Notes, Continued
Longer and Two-Part Exercises
Longer Eighth Note Exercises
Now, we can practice some longer eighth note exercises.

First, let me explain first and second endings. In this example, play the first three bars and go to the first ending. Then, play everything again from the repeat sign, but this time, skip to the the second ending. So, when you read this:

Example 1-090:

… you should actually play this:

Example 1-091:

Read these exercises:

Exercise 1-108:

"I had the chance to meet Rory Stuart as a teacher at New School for Jazz and Contemporary Music and he opened my mind and pushed my research on guitar and composition with ideas, suggestions which were seeds i can still expand and dig!"

- FRANCESCO DIODATI
(Guitarist from Italy)

"Studying rhythm with Rory Stuart was one of the most important steps in my music education. His "Rhythmic Analysis" class at New School University opened my mind up to a great number of concepts that helped me approach playing music in new and exciting ways. Even after a decade, the things I learned from Rory are as relevant as ever to the music that I play."

- CHRIS TORDINI
(Bassist, USA)

"Rory Stuart has developed such a deep understanding of rhythm that he makes the most difficult material seem easy. As his student, I had the privilege to experience challenge, a clear method, new discoveries, and fun."

- CAMILA MEZA
(Vocalist/Guitarist from Chile)

"In his Master Classes for students and teachers at Kazakh National University of Art, Rory Stuart carefully explained the basics of jazz rhythm and its development to an audience that was always engaged, tapping rhythms, singing parts, etc.... The students were inspired, and this much-anticipated workshop was so well attended that it was standing room only!"

- GULDANA ZHOLYMBETOVA
(Professor of Music, Kazakhstan)

"Rory Stuart, an internationally recognized guitarist, composer and educator, has worked with some of the foremost jazz musicians and taught many of the most important emerging young jazz stars of today. Rory has a lot of experience and information, especially in areas such as polyrhythmic compositional and improvisational techniques. He has worked long and hard to capture and convey this knowledge in this book series on rhythm, which expands the small number of works in this field. I've been waiting for these books for a long time — he knows about rhythm! It is a great contribution for all serious practitioners. Great job, Rory!"

- DR. MARCELO COEHLO
(Saxophonist and professor at Souza Lima, Sao Paolo Brazil; founder of International Rhythmic Studies Association)

"Rory's rhythm lessons opened a lot of doors for me. As a veteran player, I had spent many years focused on harmony; the lessons got me to concentrate on rhythm. Rory showed me ideas I was able to add and immediately utilize in my playing to make the music feel fresher. The lessons really influenced, and continue to influence, my playing."

- MICHAEL WOLFF
(Pianist, USA. Performed w/ Sonny Rollins, Nancy Wilson, Cal Tjader, Airto Moreira, Cannonball Adderley; coleader of Wolff & Clark Expedition)

"Endlessly organized, enthusiastic, and imaginative, Rory Stuart is one of the most gifted teachers I have ever encountered. In designing and teaching the rhythm curriculum at The New School, he has had a quiet impact on a whole generation of players in the city, and I consider myself lucky to have had the chance to study with him."

- JOHN ELLIS
(Saxophonist, USA)

This book is for you if:

- You are a beginner to music, and want to learn how to read and write rhythms.

- You are any age, an adult or young learner.

- You sing or play an instrument but never learned how music is notated (for example, perhaps you learned by ear or by imitating what a teacher played).

- You already play an instrument and read music, but want to refresh or strengthen your knowledge of rhythm notation fundamentals.

- You compose or would like to compose music or write arrangements for others, and want to be able to correctly notate it.

- You are a vocalist, play any instrument (including horns, piano, guitar, bass, strings — NOT just drums and percussion instruments!).

- You want to learn about rhythm but have not yet chosen an instrument.

- You play or want to play any style of music. This book has somewhat of an orientation towards jazz and contemporary music (funk, pop, rock, hip-hop, Afro-Cuban, Brazilian, modern classical) and includes the syncopation found in these styles of music and the swing feel of jazz. If you are an aspiring musician in a different style (e.g. folk, singer-songwriter, pre-20th century classical), you can learn what you need to know about rhythm, but the book includes some "extra" rhythmic things not usually found in your style of music.

- You are a music teacher who wants a clear progressive method to teach rhythm notation to your students.

- You are taking music classes, studying with a private instructor, or are teaching yourself.

Rhythm is the key to so much in music. When you have read this book and completed the exercises in it, you will 1) understand how rhythm is notated, 2) be able to read common rhythms in 4/4, 3) know how to write common rhythms, and 4) be prepared to study more complex rhythms.

Please note: once you have completed this book, or if you already have a solid command of the material in it, the next book for you is *THE RHYTHM BOOK – Intermediate Notation and Sight-Reading* (HL00252026).

Table of Contents

Preface

You are looking at the first in a collection of books on rhythm that have taken many years for me to complete. Perhaps you are curious as to how they came about ...

Since 1992, I have designed and taught the rhythm curriculum in the world renowned New School for Jazz and Contemporary Music in New York. I've also been musical director or teacher at jazz workshops and clinics in Europe, Asia, South America, and the USA. I've had the opportunity to teach many remarkably talented students who have gone on to do impressive things musically; but, perhaps more importantly, the wide variety of students who have come to my classes and workshops have had different musical backgrounds, different aptitudes, and different learning styles. Were it not for my experiences teaching rhythm, a subject which I think is of critical importance to the music but woefully under-represented in music education programs around the world, I would certainly never have written these books.

There are two people in particular without whose influence I would never have done the teaching that led to writing these books, and I want to acknowledge them. By way of background, let me explain that I developed into a professional jazz musician almost entirely outside of any academic setting; I took a small number of very helpful private lessons, listened to and transcribed from recordings, but largely figured out things on my own and learned "on the bandstand." Perhaps as a result of this, I had many (entirely wrong, as it turned out!) unfavorable preconceptions about teaching music. By the late 1980's, I had already been in New York City for most of the decade, had played as a sideman with many amazing musicians, and had an excellent quartet I'd put together in 1982, with a couple of critically acclaimed recordings. There were many things in life about which I was uncertain but one thing that I knew for sure was that I never wanted to be a music teacher!

The drummer in the Rory Stuart Quartet, Keith Copeland, was not only a terrific musician, but also an incredibly positive and supportive person—the kind of person one dreams about having in one's group and in one's corner. Keith was asked to do some gigs out of town and needed someone to substitute for him in teaching a class; only because the request came from him, I agreed. It turned out the class was at the New School and was about rhythm; Keith thought of me for it because of all the rhythmically unusual and challenging things we did in the Quartet. It only took one session of teaching that class to make me completely re-think everything I'd believed about teaching music. Here was a group of remarkably talented and motivated musicians from all over the world who were excited to work on everything I brought to them. Things worked out so well and I enjoyed it so much that for the next few years I became Keith's regular substitute any time he was unable to teach the class. If it were not for Keith, I would never have started teaching this rhythm class—or had the amazing experience of playing with a master drummer in my first quartet. THANKS KEITH!

In 1992, Keith was offered teaching positions in a couple of conservatories in Germany and decided to move there. The director of the New School's Jazz program, Martin Mueller, was faced with the need to get someone to replace Keith. Although I had already placed on some international critics polls, gotten 4-star reviews in Downbeat, and performed around New York, there were certainly more famous people that Martin could have recruited to teach this class. In fact, the New School jazz faculty was filled with legends of the music—the other rhythm teachers at the time were Jimmy Cobb and Chico Hamilton, and the list of faculty read like a list of "A" team jazz musicians of New York. Martin Mueller was (and still is) very attuned to everything in the program, and I suspect he had gotten positive feedback about my teaching when I substituted for Keith, but I still must give thanks to him for having the faith in me to give me a shot at teaching the class. In addition, Martin, in his rather quiet and never self-aggrandizing, but visionary way, has done a remarkable job in shaping what has certainly become one of the foremost jazz programs in the world. If it were not for Martin's giving me the opportunities he has, I would not have developed the rhythm curriculum, would not be writing this collection of books, and would not have had the extraordinary opportunity to have had all the wonderful students I have. THANKS MARTIN!

Thanks also are due to people who have helped specifically with regard to this volume: Dan Greenblatt for specific, very thoughtful feedback on some pedagogic issues, as well as tips about publication of musical instruction books; Robert Sadin for insightful suggestions; Arthur Hnatek for early feedback about some sample chapters; John Ellis and Chris Hughes for their perspectives on some notation issues; New York saxophonist Arun Luthra, a former rhythm class student who now teaches rhythm classes, in addition to his work as a performer with a diverse range of New York groups, and for discussions through the years; Tonya Bassett for her helpful comments from the perspective of a student; John Riley, who also taught some of the rhythm classes at New School after I had developed curriculum for a few years, and brought his expertise to some helpful discussions; Collin Bay and Andrew Bart for helpful feedback related to publishing; the entire team at Hal Leonard, including Keith Mardak (Chairman & CEO, first to express interest in publishing the books), Jeff Schroedl (Executive Vice President who supported me through each stage of the process), and Debbie Seeger (Production Editor); the New School for Jazz and Contemporary Music for help with funding a research assistant, and Pam Sabrin for help in applying for this funding.

Special thanks are due to that research assistant, Matt Heister. Matt has been of so much help, in many ways, with the nitty-gritty. He not only did layout/design, but also brought great ideas and feedback about musical content and presentation on so many levels—he has been a perfect combination of patience, attention to detail, and expertise in just the right combination of areas, and without him, I don't know how I would have gotten this book completed!

A generous Fulbright Scholar Award for 4 months in 2013-2014, with the support of New School, helped me get more time to work on the book during my first sabbatical in 21 years. Thank you to everyone at Fulbright who helped (special thanks to Hana Rambouskova), and to my host school Janácek Academy of Music and Performing Arts (special thanks to Vilem Spilka).

A small circle of people who are important in my life provide love and support that make everything (not just these books!) possible—thanks always to Tuck & Patti, Chris, Liz, Carole & Avery, Bob, Vaishali, and Marc!

Finally, as one who learned so much on the bandstand, I want to acknowledge that my many musical colleagues through the years contributed indirectly to this book (too many to name here, but please see my acknowledgments of them on the web), as have my hundreds of students through the years (for a small sample of them, see the Teaching page on my website www.rorystuart.com). A large number of people in the jazz world, who organize workshops and clinics and run clubs, festivals, performance spaces, and schools, are highly intelligent and capable people who could easily receive more money or fame doing other things but do what they do out of love for the music and make so many things possible; thanks to all of you! Fellow teachers and musicians around the world have also helped, especially in making me aware of the need for this book—some have gone out of their way to keep in touch and ask "when will the books be finished and published?!" Thanks!

How to Use This Book

There are 3 elements to this book: 1) the text and written examples and exercises; 2) the worksheets; and 3) the recorded examples.

As you read through the text, you will see written exercises for you to sight-read. Recordings of some of these are provided, so that you can check that you are reading them correctly. Please note the distinction between **Examples** and **Exercises** (they are numbered differently); I recommend you study both, but also practice the exercises.

A separate stack of worksheets is included on the Hal Leonard website so that you can practice writing things. Some of them are used to practice correcting notation, some are for you to create your own examples, but many are for you to transcribe recorded examples.

To access the recordings of exercises from the text, transcription examples for the worksheets, and selected examples, go to www.halleonard.com/mylibrary

Note: if you want to speed up or slow down any of the recorded exercises, you can find a number of free or inexpensive programs on the web that let you do so. You can also do this through Playback+ on the Hal Leonard website when you access the audio.

The author would be delighted to hear from you, and please write if you have questions, comments, or suggestions. To contact the author as well as to see updates, corrections, additional examples, and a forum and blog supporting the books, please visit www.RoryRhythmBooks.com

> Occasionally, there are observations that may be of interest to the teacher of rhythm to the student who wants to get into greater depth, but are not essential for the general reader. These sections are shown with a gray shaded background like you see here.

Introduction to Rhythmic Notation

Rhythmic notation and sight-reading may seem daunting at first, but can be fun to learn. I didn't learn to sight-read until I was a teen, so I remember well the problems that seemed like large hurdles at the time. One involved pitch: I remember counting ledger lines from a note on the staff I knew to one I didn't; although I couldn't recognize pitches quickly, it was immediately clear that if I spent more time doing this and memorized what pitches were written on each of the lines and spaces, it would become easy.

The other challenge was reading rhythms; at the time, this one didn't seem to have such a clear-cut solution. In fact, I have found that reading and writing rhythms is, for most people, THE single largest obstacle to becoming fluent and comfortable with notated music. After I spent some time working on reading and writing rhythms, I not only found that it all made sense, I also developed a method with which others could master this much more quickly and easily than I did. I hope you will be happily surprised by how enjoyable this is for you.

I assume you have absolutely no background and prior experience in reading rhythms. As you follow this method step-by-step, please do so at your own pace and be certain to understand each step before you move on to the next.

To move at a faster pace, skip some exercises; to move at a slower pace, if you find some of the material to be difficult, make up additional exercises of your own for each section.

Quarter Note Rhythms

As you will see, quarter note rhythms are the foundation on which you will build a solid understanding of rhythmic notation. Your mastery of quarter note rhythms will well prepare you to learn eighth note rhythms, 16th note rhythms, and the rest of the rhythmic vocabulary. Be certain you are confident with quarter note rhythms before you start on the subsequent material.

Getting Started

Begin by counting "one two three four" at a steady rate, repeating it out loud several times. How would this be written musically? Here is how your counting would be written. It is shown in two different styles in which music can be notated: **standard notation** and **rhythmic notation**.

Example 1-001 shows standard notation, which features a **treble clef** (𝄞) and **standard note heads** (●). This type of notation is used when "pitch" (how high or low the notes sound) is used in the music. Example 1-002 shows rhythmic notation, which features a **rhythm clef** (▯) and **slash note heads** (╱). The rhythm clef indicates that rhythm, but not pitch, is being used.

Example 1-001:

Example 1-002:

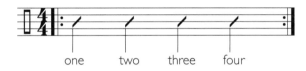

While we will be using standard notation later in the book when we introduce pitch, at this beginning stage we will not be concerning ourselves with pitch, only with rhythm. We will begin our study using rhythmic notation. We have looked at the clefs and the note heads, now let's look at each of the other elements in the above example.

The notes are placed on a **staff** - a combination of five horizontal lines separated by four spaces.

Example 1-003:

There are four notes, called **quarter notes**, in the measure (and I've written the "lyrics," one, two, three, four, underneath them).

Example 1-004:

Preceding the measure are two "4's" one above the other. This is called a **time signature**. The bottom number tells us the value of a beat; the top number tells us how many of these beats there are in a measure. In this case, the lower 4 indicates that the basic pulse we should feel is the quarter note; the upper 4 tells us that each measure lasts for a duration of four of these quarter notes. (In this book, we only examine time signatures in which the bottom number is a "4" and so the beats will always be quarter notes. Other bottom numbers, i. e., other beat values, are covered in *THE RHYTHM BOOK— Intermediate Notation and Sight-Reading.*)

Example 1-005:

There are **repeat signs** which tell us to play this measure twice (the repeat sign is the combination of the double bars and the two dots):

Example 1-006:

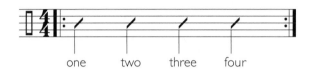

Clap on each beat as you say "one, two, three, four…" Easy, but let's make it more interesting by adding some variations!

Next, we introduce another symbol, the **quarter rest** (𝄽). It lasts as long as a quarter note, but indicates there should be silence rather than a note.

In the following exercises, continue counting "one, two, three, four" in each bar; but only clap on the beats that have quarter notes, do not clap on the beats that have quarter rests. We can describe this as "counting the time while clapping the rhythm."

Exercise 1-001:

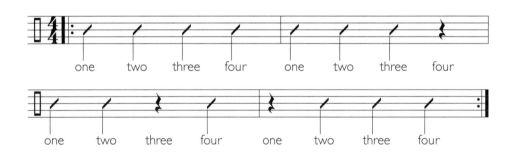

Exercise 1-002:

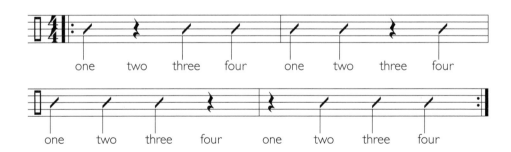

Exercise 1-003:

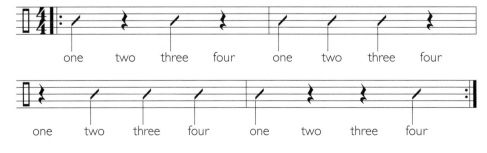

Different Ways to Do the Exercises

There is a physicality about rhythm and, right from the beginning, we want to feel the rhythm in our bodies, not just think it in our heads. Now that you've seen how quarter note rhythms look on paper, let's look at some ways you can physically play them.

Walking in Place

Try the above exercises again but, this time, walk in place as you do them. Take a step with your left foot as you say "one," right foot on "two," left foot on "three," and right foot on "four." It is easy and natural for an activity such as walking to be done at a steady rhythmic pace so it helps you get in a groove. Keep stepping on every beat, whether it has a note or a rest, but only clap when there is a note. The steady walking will serve as your "metronome." Try the next exercise in the same way:

Exercise 1-004:

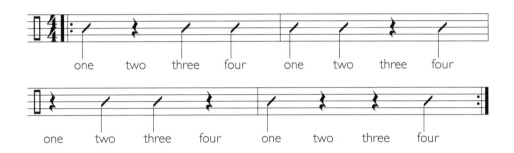

Now, do Exercise 1-004, exactly as you did it before, but do not count out loud. Count "one, two, three, four" in your mind, but walk in place and clap the rhythm.

Singing the Rhythm While Clapping Quarter Notes

Now, instead of counting the time while we clap the rhythm, we will sing the rhythm while clapping quarter notes. Clap on every beat (one, two, three, four) and sing the rhythm that is written (for example, sing the syllable "dah" each place there is a quarter note written, and do not sing anything where there is a rest). You can continue walking in place as you did before (walking is optional, try doing this with and without walking in place).

Exercise 1-005:

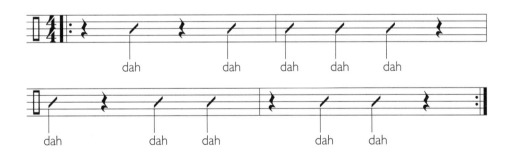

Try using syllables other than "dah"—whatever feels good musically to you. You can also sing beat numbers instead of the syllable "dah." Singing numbers at first can be useful, as it helps you keep track of where you are. As you become an experienced sight-reader, you will stop consciously thinking the number "four" when playing a note on the fourth beat.

> Opinions about the importance of singing beat numbers vary: some feel it adds a "non-musical" step in the process that makes reading more difficult (I tend to have students move away from this rather quickly)—but others have students stick with it for longer (my colleague Arun Luthra advocates this strongly, feeling it is like a baseball player warming up by swinging two bats).

Exercise 1-006 shows how Exercise 1-005 would be performed singing beat numbers.

Exercise 1-006:

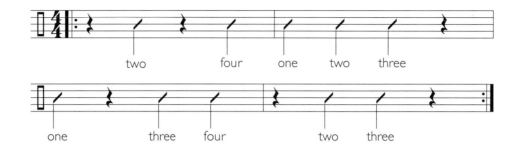

You have already tried a few variations: counting all the quarter notes while you clap the written rhythm; "walking" the quarter notes while you clap the written rhythm (with and without simultaneously counting the quarter notes out loud); and clapping all the quarter notes (with and without simultaneously "walking" them) while you sing the written rhythm. Try one more variation on Exercise 1-005: don't clap at all - just sing the rhythm while you walk quarter notes.

Here is a table of these variations:

Sing/Speak	Clap	Walk	
Quarter notes	Rhythm	(none)	(we did this for Exercise 1-001- Exercise 1-003)
Quarter notes	Rhythm	Quarter notes	(we did this for Exercise 1-004)
(none)	Rhythm	Quarter notes	(first variation we did on Exercise 1-004)
Rhythm	Quarter notes	(none)	(we did this for Exercise 1-005)
Rhythm	Quarter notes	Quarter notes	(we did this also for Exercise 1-005)
Rhythm	(none)	Quarter notes	(our most recent variation for Exercise 1-005)

Are any of these variations difficult for you? It is good for all of them to feel steady and easy. If any are difficult, practice them with the following exercises until they become easy.

Exercise 1-007:

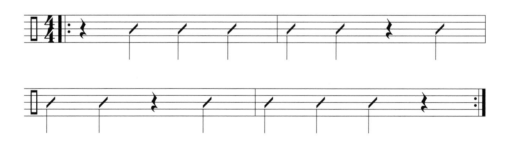

Exercise 1-008:

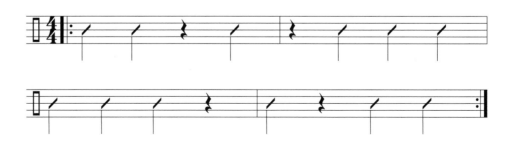

Exercise 1-009:

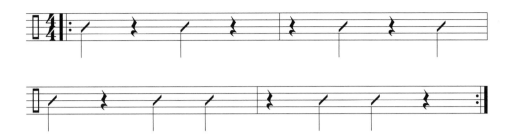

> Notice that when we clap or tap quarter notes, the notes always sound short; when we sing them or play them on some instruments, such as wind instruments, we have a choice between sustaining the notes for their full duration or playing them at the correct time but making them short.

Clapping on "One & Three" or "Two & Four"

Our goal right now is to continue getting greater confidence, ease, and flexibility in reading quarter note rhythms. Next, we will see what it is like to sing written rhythms while we clap. But, we will not clap every quarter note. First, we will try clapping on "one" and "three:"

Exercise 1-010:

…while we sing the rhythm in this exercise (which also shows the "clap" below each beat one and three). Try singing "dah" on each written note, or sing the number of the beat it's on, and see which works best for you. In either case, sing only where there is a note, don't sing anything where there is a written rest:

Exercise 1-011:

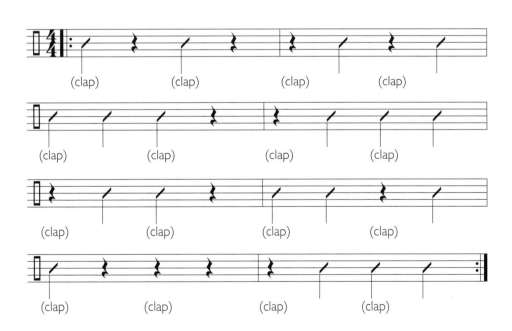

If you found that exercise too difficult, practice it two bars at a time. Repeat two bars, memorizing them and grooving, then do the same with the next two bars. Then practice putting together these two bar sections until you can play the entire exercise without stopping. Use this same approach when necessary with any of the following exercises.

Let's try singing a rhythm while we clap on "two" and "four." First, we get the "two" and "four" groove happening. Sing "one, two, three, four" while clapping on "two" and "four" ("one, two, three, four" is our countoff; it does not mean you have to sing the number each note is on in the following exercise, you can sing "dah"):

Exercise 1-012:

...and continue clapping on "two" and "four" while you sing the following:

Exercise 1-013:

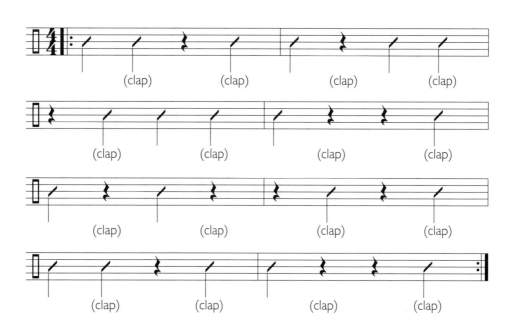

Are either of these clapping patterns (clapping on "one" and "three" or clapping on "two" and "four") more difficult for you? If so, choose some of the exercises you've done already and try singing them with that clapping pattern. At first, some people find clapping on "two" and "four" to be more difficult, and it is especially important to be comfortable doing this in order to feel many of the styles of music we will discuss.

Tapping Your Foot
We will add a variation now. Tap your foot on beat "one" of every measure, while you clap on "two" and "four." Once you have this physically on "auto-pilot," keep doing it while you sing the following exercise:

Exercise 1-014:

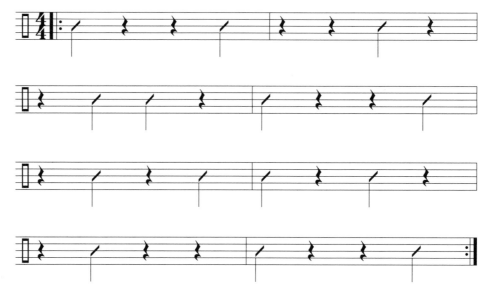

This may seem tricky at first—after all, you're singing one thing, clapping a second thing, and foot-tapping a third thing!— but do it several times, and you will find it gets easier with practice.

> Although you sing the written notes and remain silent during the rests, be sure to feel each beat of rest internally, especially where there are consecutive quarter rests. Some people find an exercise like this to be easier if they sing a different syllable—try singing "dee" instead of "dah" for example.

Do Exercise 1-014 again, but this time clapping your hands on "one" each measure, and tapping your feet on "two" and "four."

> Try the different ways of tapping I've described, gain some flexibility, but then concentrate on the ways that work best for you.
>
> An interesting aside about tapping among jazz musicians is that some great players insist that one should tap on "2" and "4," others insist on "1" and "3," and the late Cannonball Adderley, who had one of the best time feels I've ever heard, never visibly tapped at all. Joe Lovano did a master class for my department in which he spoke of being able to tap in many different ways, and demonstrated how each way he tapped caused him to improvise a bit differently rhythmically.

Finally, let's try one more clapping pattern, while you read and sing rhythms. First, practice clapping only on beat "three" each measure, while you sing "one, two, three, four:"

Exercise 1-015:

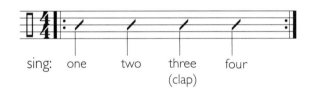

...once you are comfortable doing that, continue clapping while you sing the following exercise:

Exercise 1-016:

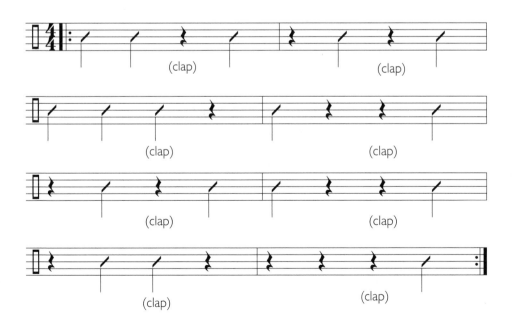

In order to practice hearing and transcribing some examples like the ones you have been reading, try transcribing the dictation examples on Worksheet 1-W-001.

Feeling the Pulse

Once you are comfortable with what we have done so far, you can take the next step: feel the constant quarter note pulse inside (you can still walk in place if you want), but only clap the rhythm. Try doing that with the following exercise:

Exercise 1-017:

With the following exercise, do not clap. Just feel the quarter note pulse inside (walk in place if you want) and sing the written rhythm:

Exercise 1-018:

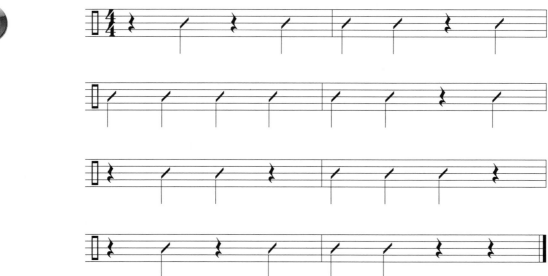

If you find either of these (only clapping the rhythm, or only singing it) to be difficult for you, go back and practice this with the exercises we have already done in this chapter.

Note Density

Most people find it easier to read more notes rather than fewer (another way to say this is that they find it easier to read notes than rests). Below are two exercises—the first one with many notes, the second with fewer. Try performing these in a couple of the ways we've tried already (for example, sing the rhythms while tapping your foot on "2" and "4"). Notice which of the two exercises you find easier.

Many notes:

Exercise 1-019:

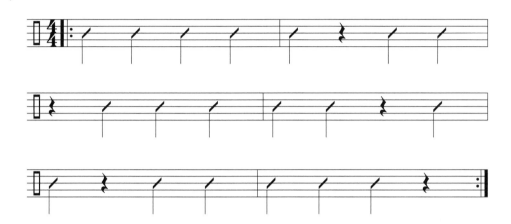

Fewer notes:

Exercise 1-020:

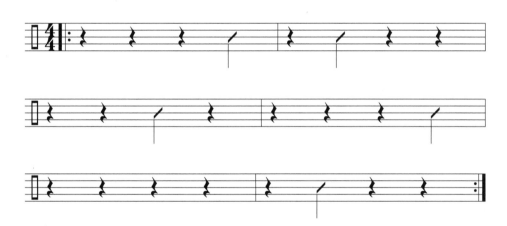

Based on what you've observed about what is most easy or difficult for you, try creating a couple of your own exercises. First, create one that uses what you find easy. Then, create one that you find more difficult. Sing and clap what you have written. Use Worksheet 1-W-002.

Extending Note Durations

So far, we have worked on reading rhythms in which all of the notes and rests each last for exactly one beat. This might be all we would need if we were playing an instrument (such as a wood block or cowbell) that did not allow for the possibility of sustaining a note. But most instruments, including the human voice, allow a note to be sustained. In order to indicate how long the notes are to be held, we need to introduce a few symbols in addition to the quarter note and the quarter rest.

Half Notes

Here is the **half note** (♩)—it is sustained for two beats—followed by a **half rest** (▬)—which means there is silence for two beats:

Example 1-007:

Doo _____

While clapping "one, two, three, four," sing the sound "Doo" in the above example, sustaining it for the first two beats. Then, leave silence for the next two beats, as you continue clapping. Like the quarter note, the half note can be stemmed up or down; but its note head is left empty, while the note head of the quarter note is filled in.

A half note written in standard notation (rather than rhythmic notation) looks like this:

Example 1-008:

Sing the following exercises. Notice that in each example, you sing the notes in the second bar on the same beats as those in the first bar. But one note in the second bar of each example is sustained longer than it was in the first bar.

Exercise 1-021:

Exercise 1-022:

Exercise 1-023:

Exercise 1-024:

Exercise 1-025:

Exercise 1-026:

Exercise 1-027:

Exercise 1-028:

Try singing the following exercise, which incorporates half notes, while clapping "one, two, three, four:"

Exercise 1-029:

Check to be sure you are doing it correctly—for example, in the first measure, you sing a note on beat "one," then sing a note on beat "two" that you sustain through beat "three," then sing another note on "four."

Here is another exercise to sing, using half notes. Try singing it while clapping in different ways:

- clapping on "one, two, three, four"
- clapping only on "one" and "three"
- clapping only on "two" and "four"

Exercise 1-030:

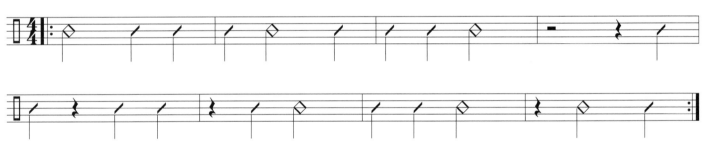

Whole Notes

Just as a half note lasts twice as long as a quarter note (two beats instead of one), a **whole note** (◇) lasts twice as long as a half note (four beats instead of two). Since it fills the entire bar in the 4/4 meter, there is only one thing that can happen: the whole note starts on beat "one" and sustains for the entire measure:

Example 1-009:

Ah _____

A whole note written in standard notation (rather than rhythmic notation) looks like this:

Example 1-010:

Just as we can have a whole note, we can have a **whole rest** (━), which simply indicates silence for all four beats of the bar. Notice that the only difference between the symbol for the whole rest and that for the half rest is where they are placed: the whole rest is generally placed immediately underneath the fourth line from the bottom of the staff, and the half rest is placed just above the middle line:

Example 1-011:

Dotted Half Notes
There are only two more note value symbols that you need to know for now.
The first one is a **dotted half note** (◇·). The dotted half note lasts for a total of three beats:

Example 1-012:

...and the second one is the **dotted half rest** (━··)

Example 1-013:

Please note, however, that professional music copyists generally do not dot half rests in 4/4 so, they would write the previous example as:

Example 1-014:

Read the following and notice that in each exercise all bars have notes that are sung on the same beats. But, in the last bar of both examples, the note is sustained using the dotted half note:

Exercise 1-031:

13

Exercise 1-032:

Since we have introduced the dot, here is a word of explanation about it. When a dot follows a note head or rest, it increases the duration of that note or rest by one half. In the example of the dotted half note, a half note normally lasts for two beats, so a dotted half note lasts half again as long (one beat extra) for a total of three beats.

Now we know symbols that represent music of one, two, three, and four beats in 4/4, or in any other meter where the bottom number is "4":

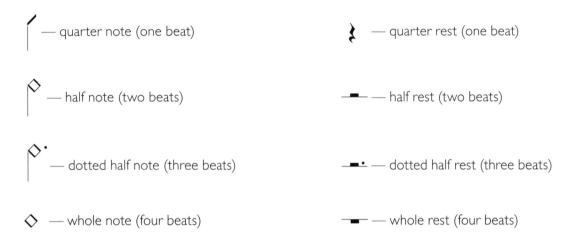

Let's practice reading some rhythms that have extended note durations and use the symbols we've just learned. In these, and all future exercises, get the most out of your practice by implementing any/all of the performance variations we've previously discussed.

Exercise 1-033:

Exercise 1-034:

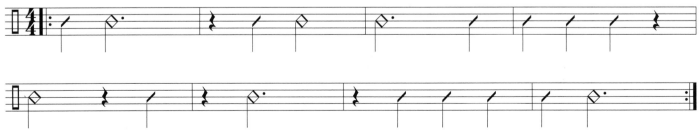

Exercise 1-035:

Exercise 1-036:

Exercise 1-037:

Try transcribing the dictation examples on Worksheet 1-W-003.

The Tie

It turns out that, with the symbols we have discussed, we can represent almost anything that can happen rhythmically at the quarter note level. But what if a note is sustained from the end of one bar through the beginning of the next bar? There is a simple solution, and it is called the **tie** (⌒). When two notes are connected with a "tie," we sing or play the first note for its duration, then continue to sustain it through the duration of the second note (we do not play the second note separately as we would if it were not tied).

It is important for clarity that you always connect the note heads (NOT the stems!) with the tie marking.

In each of these exercises, we sing notes on the same beats in bars 3 and 4 as in bars 1 and 2 — but, in bars 3 and 4, there is a note sustained (tied across the barline) instead of a rest. A double bar line separates the two versions.

Exercise 1-038:

Exercise 1-039:

Exercise 1-040:

Exercise 1-041:

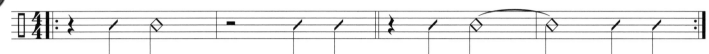

Exercise 1-042:

Exercise 1-043:

Exercise 1-044:

We previously noted that it is usually easier to read notes than rests. But, when it comes to sustained notes with ties, many people find it is more difficult to read the sustained notes than it is to read short notes with rests. Don't worry if you find it tricky at first to read ties—continue practicing it until it becomes comfortable.

Transcribe the dictation examples on Worksheet 1-W-004.

A First Look at Required Beats

Perhaps it occurred to you that, by using ties, you could have written everything we've done so far by using only quarter notes, quarter rests, and ties. You may even think that half notes, dotted halves and whole notes create unnecessary complications, and that instead of this:

Example 1-015:

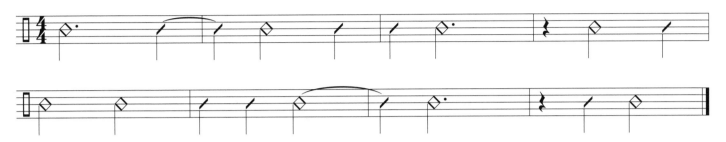

…it would be better to notate like this:

Example 1-016:

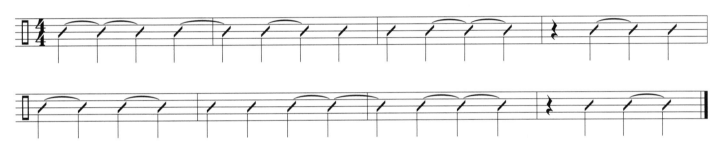

It is true that these two examples sound exactly the same. However, if you prefer the second way, with many quarter notes tied, please take my word for it that more experienced sightreaders prefer the first way instead and that, with experience, you will too.

In fact, there is a system of principles for the best way to write rhythms. What do they say about quarter note rhythms in 4/4? Most concisely: "When writing rhythms in 4/4 at the quarter note level, never use any ties except between bars." These are not "rules just for the sake of rules" but rather an easy system that is very helpful both for the writer and the sight-reader.

Another way to think about this, which will make more sense as we apply these principles to rhythms at different rates, is that we must always "show the required beats"; the only "required beat" to show in 4/4 in quarter note level rhythms is beat "one."

For now, think of a required beat as one that we must "show" (see represented by a note or rest on the page). To understand what we mean by "showing" a beat, notice that, in the following example, we "show" beat two, but do not "show" beat three:

Example 1-017:

In General:

• Do not show unrequired beats when you do not need to. You might also describe this in this way: write the least possible as long as you show the required beats (thus, at the quarter note level, use half notes, dotted halves, or whole notes, rather than tying quarter notes within the bar).

• Always be certain to show the required beats (do not worry about this for now, as there is no way at the quarter note level not to show beat "one").

…But, when you consider the implications of these, they boil down to *"No ties, except between bars."* for quarter note level rhythms in 4/4.

I find it can help solidify understanding if you practice correcting something that is poorly notated. For example, take something that is poorly notated like this:

Example 1-018:

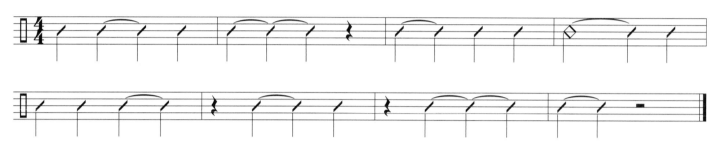

… and correct it using the principle we discussed, so that it looks like this:

Example 1-019:

 Try correcting the poorly written examples on Worksheet 1-W-005.

Possibilities for Quarter Note Level Rhythms in 4/4

You have already read many of the possible rhythms that can happen in a bar of 4/4 with quarter note level rhythms. If we think of this as a "language," it is one that has a small "vocabulary." Let's look at every possible figure that can happen in a bar of 4/4. First, here is the entire vocabulary if we sustain each note until the next note happens or the bar ends:

Example 1-020:

As you see, there are only 16 possible rhythms that can happen in a bar – even if we include a bar of total silence in the list of possibilities. Be sure that you are very comfortable with each of these.

If we make some of the notes shorter, there are a few more ways we can write things. For example, if we have the figure with two notes, one on each of the first two beats, we wrote it above as:

Example 1-021:

…but it could also be written in two ways with the second note shorter:

Example 1-022:

If we list every possibility, including all the variations in note durations, there are still only 34 — here they are:

Example 1-023:

There is absolutely no reason to remember the number of possibilities — either 16 with sustained notes, or 34 including all the possibilities with shorter duration — the important thing is to be completely comfortable and familiar with each of these rhythms.

> If you understand how the notation system works, in principle there is no need to memorize anything — but, if you want to, there are very few rhythms to memorize. You will keep seeing these rhythms again and again, and find that they become effortless to read or write. The more familiar you become with them, the less you will have to figure out when you read.

Here is a quarter note level exercise to read, using the rhythms you have learned:

Exercise 1-045:

...and another:

Exercise 1-046:

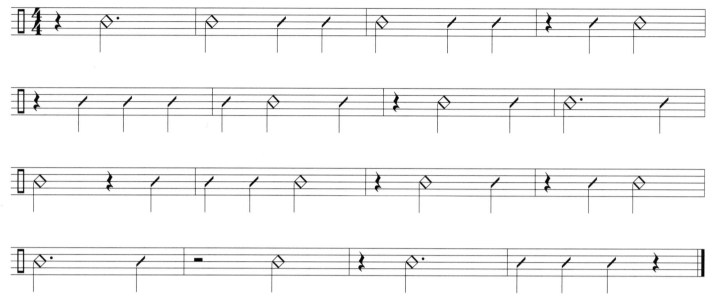

 Transcribe more dictation examples, paying special attention to try to hear and accurately write the duration of each note. Use Worksheet 1-W-006.

Count Offs and Pickups

We now know the entire language of quarter note level rhythms. What might we want to do with this language? We can create and write a rhythm; read and sing or perform a rhythm ourselves; or hear and write a rhythm someone else has played. We can practice with a friend, singing a rhythm for them to write, then notating a rhythm they sing to us.

Count Offs

Whether performing with others, or singing a rhythm for our friend to practice writing, there is a skill we need that is important, but that many people take for granted: we need to be able to do a count off. If you have been doing the dictation practice examples, you've heard count offs preceding each example.

The count off shows others what the tempo is and when the music begins. If they are reading music, it tells them when to begin reading their part; if they are practicing rhythmic notation, it shows them where the time is and where the first bar in your example begins.

From the point of view of the person who hears your count off, the tempo must be clear, and it must be obvious where the count off ends and the written music begins (both of these would also be important if a band were starting a piece of music together, even if they were not reading it).

If you are not already very strong at count offs, here are a few suggestions. Imagine, for the upcoming examples, that you are counting off a piece of music for a band.

Tempo

We do not want to count the piece off either too fast or too slow. We also do not want the count off to feel unsteady (the tempo getting faster or slower, or fluctuating inconsistently while we are counting it off). The secret to a steady count off at the right tempo is to get the tempo very strong in your mind and body before you count it off.

"Play" a few bars of the music in your head exactly where you want it. Silently "groove." Perhaps begin to snap your fingers at just that tempo (snap on "two" and "four" unless the music is very slow, in which case you can snap on "one," "two," "three," "four.") Then count out loud at exactly the tempo you are hearing in your head. You can record yourself doing this, and evaluate how clear and steady you are making your count offs, and whether they are at exactly the tempo you want. Even better, do this count off for someone else and see whether they find it to be clear.

Duration of the count off

We also want to make sure the band knows when to begin—so they need to know how long your count off will be before they should start to play. One solution to this is to always tell them this before you begin—for example: "I will count off two bars of 4/4."

For 4/4 count offs, there is a standard approach, which allows you to make this clear without having to tell the band anything beforehand. Use this count off:

Example 1-024:

Practice singing some of the examples we have done already, including ones you have made up, preceding them with this count off. Set up the tempo first in your mind, groove to it, then say the count off with confidence. Try recording yourself doing this, and see how strong and clear you are making both the count off and the example you sing.

For example, try doing this exercise (I have actually written in the count off — normally you would not see a count off written in!):

Exercise 1-047:

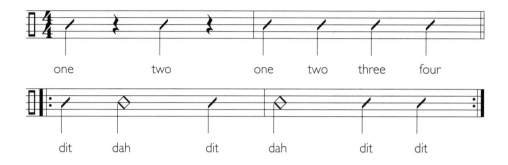

Notice that, in the above exercise, I put some syllables to the notes you sang in the example. But, you do not have to sing it, you could also say the count off, then clap the example.

Also practice feeling the groove of someone else who is counting off a tune, and locking immediately into that groove when you play. Record yourself performing with a friend and notice, after their count off, how you play in the first few measures of the tune; notice any problematic tendencies you have (coming in too fast or slow in general, or problems on tunes with certain feels or tempos). Work on correcting them – continuing to record yourself to verify your success at this.

Pickups

Pickups or "pickup notes" are notes that are played before the first bar of music. In every example we have done so far, the rhythms we sing or clap always have begun after the count off (although they do not always begin on beat "one" — some began on a beat after that). In some music, the first notes are played before the count off is completed (i.e. before the entire band comes in).

> Examples of melodies that begin with pickups are "Happy Birthday," "When the Saints Go Marching In" or standards such as "Autumn Leaves" and "There Is No Greater Love." (By contrast, "Jingle Bells" starts right on beat "one" with no pickup.)

The notation of pickups is a very special case. We need to make it clear that the pickup notes happen before the first bar of music. We do this in two ways: 1) we do not precede the pickup notes by rests; and 2) we indicate the start of the first bar of music, either with a double bar line or, if appropriate, a repeat sign.

> In the classical world, the term for a pickup is "anacrusis." In music at faster rates than quarter notes and eighth notes, there is more to be said (see THE RHYTHM BOOK — Intermediate Notation and Sight-Reading) but, for now, just follow this rule: "Do not put any rests before the first note in a pickup."

24

Here is an exercise in which there are pickup notes:

Exercise 1-048:

The double bar line is placed after the pickup notes:

Since the pickup is only two beats long, and we do not precede it with rests, the first bar (called the "pickup bar") has fewer than the four beats a normal bar of 4/4 music would.

> How does it work to perform this example with a count off? If you are playing the written music on an instrument that is not a wind instrument (so that, unlike playing a trumpet, saxophone, trombone, etc., you can speak and play at the same time), you could say the complete count off as usual, but start playing notes on your instrument during the last two beats of the count off. However, if you are singing, or playing a wind instrument, you have to stop saying the count off once you begin playing the pickup.

In this exercise, we sing some syllables to distinguish the count off from the music:

Exercise 1-049:

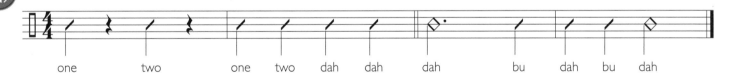

An alternative count off for Exercise 1-049 would be counting every beat in the first bar and the two beats before the pickup in the second bar: "one, two, three, four, one, two." The disadvantage is that it is not consistent with how we have been doing other count offs, and there is even a risk that musicians will start playing the pickup in the first bar; the advantage of it is that it makes it easier to clearly convey the tempo, which you get more chance to express.

Here is another exercise—this time, the pickup precedes a two bar section that is repeated:

Exercise 1-050:

You may have noticed that, in the previous exercise, the last three beats of the music that is repeated sounds the same as the pickup. This does not have to be so, as we see in another exercise:

Exercise 1-051:

It is also possible that a pickup may be tied into the first bar of music:

Exercise 1-052:

Here are some more exercises with pickups for you to practice singing:

Exercise 1-053:

Exercise 1-054:

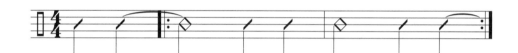

Exercise 1-055:

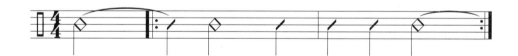

Exercise 1-056:

 When you transcribe a rhythm, it's important to be aware of where it falls with respect to the count off. Practice this, transcribing the examples in Worksheet 1-W-007 and Worksheet 1-W-008. Also, try Group-Exercises on Worksheet 1-W-009, Worksheet 1-W-010 and Worksheet 1-W-011.

More Performance Variations

You have already performed exercises by singing or clapping the written rhythms, and using counting, foot tapping, walking, clapping (on all or selected beats)—or nothing but your inner sense of groove—to keep track of the quarter note pulse. Here are a few more variations to try:

• In each of the variations we tried previously in which there was clapping, replace the clapping with tapping with one hand perhaps on your thigh or on a table or chair.

• Try tapping the written rhythm with one hand while you tap on "two" and "four" with the other hand.

• Snap your fingers on "two" and "four" while you walk quarter notes and sing the rhythm.

• Snap your fingers on "two" and "four" while you tap your foot on "one" and "three" and sing the rhythm.

• Snap your fingers on "two" and "four" while you tap your foot on beat "one" only and sing the rhythm.

• Only after all the singing, clapping, tapping, and other variations are very comfortable and you're feeling confident in reading the rhythms should you try playing them on your instrument. Try this while tapping your feet in the different ways described previously, or without any foot tapping. If you play a pitched instrument, choose one note and play the rhythms repeating only that note. If you are a singer, choose a single pitch to sing and repeat that pitch in singing the exercises. If you are a percussionist, play them on a single drum. Later, we will discuss what to do next on your instrument.

> Those who teach this material may have strong feelings about the order in which to introduce the performance variations. If you are a teacher, experiment and see what works best in your classes. Students differ in what comes most easily to them; if you are a student, I suggest you try the different variations and see what works best for you, progressing to more difficult variations as you master those you find easy.

The Transcription Process

If you have been using this book as the text for a class, you have no doubt already begun to practice not only singing examples, but also transcribing examples sung by others. But, if you are using it on your own and have not done the dictation examples, you may not yet have practiced writing down things you hear.

You may find that writing down an example you hear is nearly as easy as singing one that you read—or you might find it quite a bit more difficult at first. This seems to vary from person to person—and I work with some students who, although good at reading rhythms, are not nearly as good at writing them at first.

 Before continuing, try a couple of the examples from Worksheet 1-W-012, and notice the process you are using. It can help to be aware of the steps involved in the transcription process. These may be invisible to you at first if you find yourself able to hear and immediately notate an example correctly. But, by being aware of the process, you can notice if there is any step that causes you difficulty. This self-observation is very helpful because once you notice the step that is a problem, you can practice in a way to specifically get better at that step.

Here is the transcription process, as I see it:

1) Hear the rhythm and correctly hear how it relates to the beat.

2) Sing the rhythm back in your mind repeatedly, remembering it accurately.

3) In your mind, slow the tempo of the example as much as you need to without changing the rhythm or its relationship to the beat.

4) Identify the rate of notes—on what "grid" is the example (in the examples we have done so far, if you tap quarter notes, every note would fall on one of the quarter notes in each bar, so we would call this a "quarter note grid").

5) Notice how the notes fall bar-by-bar (what notes are in the first bar, second bar, etc.). Then, notice how they fall beat-by-beat.

6) Write the rhythms, using this beat-by-beat awareness. (Make sure that, in doing this, you do not change the rhythm you have been singing repeatedly in your mind)

7) Confirm that you have done things correctly notation-wise: are there the correct number of beats written in each bar? Have you followed notation principles we have discussed?

8) Read what you have written as though you had never before seen it. Confirm that what you have written sounds exactly like the thing you are transcribing. If not, repeat any stages in this process as needed to make the correction.

If you find that any of the stages in this process cause you difficulties, spend some focused practice time just on those stages. For example, if you have trouble immediately and accurately remembering a rhythm you hear, take very small excerpts from any recording, listen to them once, sing them back immediately several times, then listen once more, singing along, to confirm you remembered correctly. As you get better at this, gradually progress to longer and trickier excerpts. Notice that, in isolating this part of the process, you can improve at it without even notating anything.

For another example, if you have trouble slowing the example down without altering it, practice just that: take a small excerpt from a recording, sing it back at tempo, then sing it slightly slower, then again at the original tempo (periodically check that you are still singing it as you heard it originally). Repeat this, singing it slightly slower every time, while checking that you are still singing it accurately.

 Try transcribing more dictation examples, noticing the process you are using and which stages in the process are most challenging to you. Use Worksheet 1-W-012.

In addition to the examples you have just transcribed, if possible, also work on things with a friend: one of you sings an example, which the other transcribes. Alternate who sings and who transcribes. Use some examples from this book, but, to make it more fun, also create a few of your own examples before you get together.

Eighth Note Rhythms
Introduction to Eighth Notes

We have been working with quarter notes, which each take one beat; eighth notes are twice as fast—they divide each beat into two. If you count "one, two, three, four" as you have before, but squeeze an "and" in between each, you will be counting eighth notes:

Example 1-025:

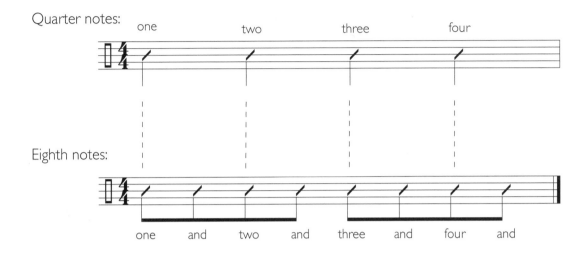

Say these two bars, making sure that the "one, two, three, four" sounds at exactly the same rate in each, and the "and" divides each beat evenly in the 2nd bar:

Exercise 1-057:

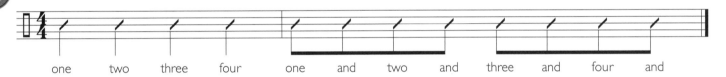

Notice that the eighth notes in the above exercise look just like the quarter notes except they are beamed together.

The beam connects the note stems, whether the stems point up or down:

Example 1-026:

We can also show that an individual note is an eighth note without beaming it to another note by using a flag. Important note: flags always point "forward" (to the right) of the note, regardless of whether the notes are stemmed up or down:

Example 1-027:

Here is an **eighth rest** (). When writing these by hand, it is especially important to make the distinction between your eighth rest and quarter rest very obvious, so that the person reading the music does not have to put any energy into determining which you mean:

Example 1-028:

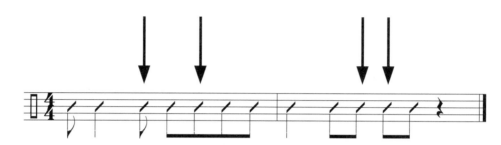

This leaves us with one notation question to answer: when should we leave an eighth note completely unbeamed, and use a flag instead (see first arrow, below), when should we beam it to eighth notes on each side of it (see second arrow), and when should we leave it beamed only to the eighth note that precedes it (see third arrow) or follows it (see fourth arrow)?

Example 1-029:

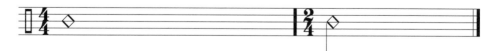

Before we answer that question, we look at the relationship between eighth note rhythms and the quarter note rhythms with which we are already familiar.

From Quarter Note Level to Eighth Note Level

For every rhythm at the quarter note level we have learned already, there is a corresponding rhythm (played twice as fast with respect to the count off) at the eighth note level. As soon as you understand this relationship between the quarter note figures in 4/4 and their corresponding eighth note figures in 2/4, you will realize there is not a lot of new vocabulary to learn—you just need to familiarize yourself with how these familiar rhythms look when written twice as fast.

As you'll notice, we are introducing a new time signature, 2/4. As you might guess, it is exactly like 4/4 except it lasts for only two quarter note pulses instead of four quarter note pulses.

An important point when you are first learning these eighth note rhythms is that you do not have to do them quickly—they only have to sound twice as fast with respect to the tempo set in the count off. This means that, at first, it is fine to make your count offs half as fast as they were at quarter level, so the figures will sound exactly the same as the quarter note figures you already know, but you will get familiar both with the new relationship to the count off and with how the figures are written at the eighth note level.

Let's revisit each figure that can happen at the quarter note level (first the "sustained version") and see its corresponding eighth note figure. Notice how simple this is: we take half the value of each note, and beam everywhere we can (with the next to last example, we have a couple choices). Here is each quarter note figure followed by its corresponding eighth note figure:

Example 1-030:

Notice in the following example that we put a dot after the quarter note. Just as dotting a half note adds half again its value (so a dotted half note is as long as a half note tied to a quarter note) dotting a quarter note adds half again its value. Thus, a quarter note is as long as two eighth notes, so a dotted quarter is as long three eighth notes (i.e. as long as a quarter note tied to an eighth note).

Example 1-031:

Example 1-032:

Top music copyists, when they are writing eighth-note-level music in 4/4, do not dot quarter rests; instead, they separately write quarter rest and eighth rest, as in the following example. This does not seem logical—why dot quarter notes but not dot quarter rests?—but this is common practice.

Example 1-033:

Example 1-034:

Example 1-035:

Example 1-036:

Example 1-037:

Example 1-038:

Example 1-039:

Example 1-040:

Example 1-041:

Example 1-042:

Example 1-043:

Example 1-044:

Note that the next to last example could also have been written this way:

Example 1-045:

…and the last bar of Example 1-044 could have been written with all four eighth notes beamed together. We will discuss beaming alternatives later.

First, try singing each eighth note figure by itself with a slow count off, so it sounds like the familiar quarter note figure that precedes it. Next, try singing each pair of figures, keeping the pulse constant, so the eighth note figure sounds twice as fast as the corresponding quarter note figure that precedes it.

You can sing the names of the beats (some people find this helpful).

Exercise 1-058:

… or sing syllables of your choice, for example:

Exercise 1-059:

… or clap the rhythms.

Now you can try all the performance variations we worked on previously: walk quarter notes while you do this, sing quarter notes while you clap the rhythm, or clap quarter notes while you sing the rhythm.

Practice converting between quarter note level figures and their corresponding eighth note level figures in 2/4: Worksheet 1-W-013.

Possibilities for Eighth Note Rhythms in 2/4

We have already seen every eighth note rhythm that can happen in a bar of 2/4 if we sustain the notes. If we list every possibility, including all the variations with shorter note durations, here are all of them:

Example 1-046:

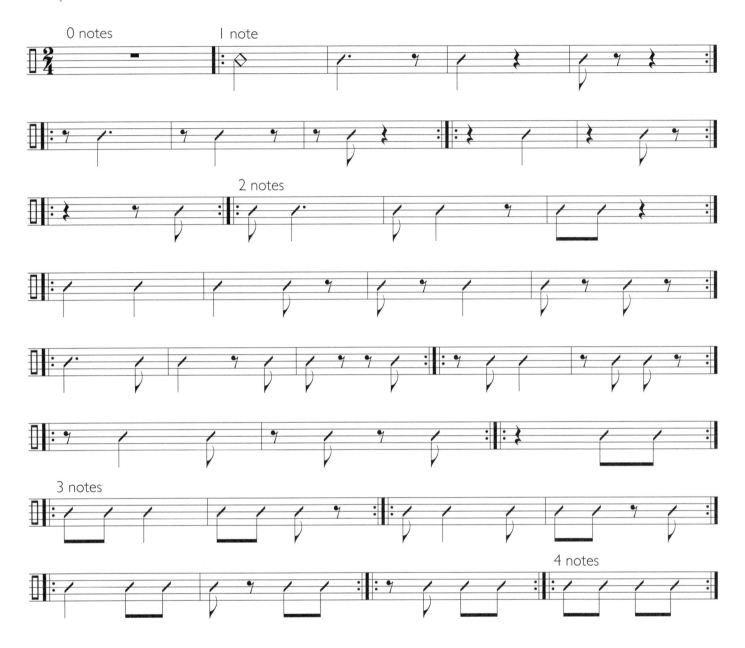

Like our list of 34 figures that can happen in 4/4 at the quarter note level, these 34 figures at the eighth note level in 2/4 are the entire "vocabulary" of the "language." Where we are not trying to be very precise about the duration of notes (for example, because the tempo is very fast, or the instrument for which we are writing does not have precise control of note duration), we tend to favor the version of each figure where the note values are written longer. They are easier to read because there are fewer things written in the bar. We would be especially unlikely to use any of the versions in which there are eighth rests on the offbeats (the "ands"). Also, as we shall see soon, there is an articulation mark (the staccato mark) that can make a note written long sound shorter, so, even if we want the notes to sound short, we can maintain this "fewer things written in the bar" style.

How to Beam Eighth Notes

For a moment, let's return to the question we posed in Example 1-029 on page 30 about how to beam eighth notes. A well notated bar of 4/4 should look like two well notated bars of 2/4 without the bar line between them. In 4/4, we need to beam each bar as though it were two well-beamed bars of 2/4 — and never beam between these two imaginary bars of 2/4. This is the first unambiguous rule: we NEVER beam from the second beat to the third beat in 4/4. Since we want the bar of 4/4 to look like two well-notated bars of 2/4, for the remaining decisions, we must understand how best to beam eighth notes in a bar of 2/4. The second unambiguous rule is that we always beam eighth notes that are part of the same beat.

So, the second rules says always write this:

Example 1-047:

...and never this:

Example 1-048:

Incidentally, there is only one place where I see this rule violated: in music for vocalists that has lyrics written in:

Example 1-049:

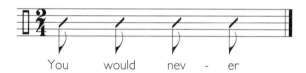

I believe this older style of notation for vocalists may be based on the belief that it is easier to see each syllable of the lyrics if the corresponding note is unbeamed; however, I wonder whether it has also been considered acceptable because vocal music (in standards, pop tunes, etc…) has often been rhythmically fairly simple. If you want to use the old style in writing vocal music, there is only one rule you need to know: "Do not beam ANYTHING"! Many jazz vocalists I know far prefer to see eighth notes beamed in the way we are spelling out.

The remainder of our discussion only addresses the "instrumental" approach to beaming.

With the remaining beaming decisions there are some possibilities to consider. In common practice there is agreement about one more thing — let's call this the third rule — we do not beam between beats if neither of the beats themselves have beams.

So, we would never beam this way:

Example 1-050:

But, what should we do instead? The best choice would be to use the staccato mark here. The staccato mark indicates that the note is to be performed shorter than its full duration. We often write a quarter note with a staccato mark instead of an eighth note followed by an eighth rest, so that there are fewer things in the bar and it is easier to read. For a full discussion of the staccato, see page 51. Incorporating the staccato, this could best be written:

Example 1-051:

Sometimes, some would beam the entire two beats; probably not as good a choice, but one that we see sometimes in common practice:

Example 1-052:

Notice a small detail: when beaming the rests, we have the choice to put what are sometimes called "half stems" to the rests. With "half stems," the previous example would look like this:

Example 1-053:

Let's look at another example. Here is a good way to write this:

Example 1-054:

Might we see it written any other way in common practice? Yes, we sometimes see:

Example 1-055:

... and sometimes like this:

Example 1-056:

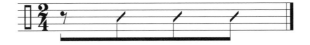

Of course we would NEVER see it written this way by someone with a good understanding of beaming:

Example 1-057:

... and that is made clear by the third rule. In the above example, the two eighth notes of beat 2 are not beamed (this already violates our second rule!), therefore we should not beam between the beats.

Although, in common practice we might see things as they are written in Example 1-052, Example 1-055, and Example 1-056, the best way to notate these are shown in Example 1-051 and Example 1-054. To always write things this way, we would follow a set of beaming rules that is more strict.

This more stringent set, encompassing everything we have discussed, is beautifully and clearly stated by my colleague Arun Luthra as: "Eighth notes in 4/4 should only be beamed in 4s or 2s to avoid them being mistaken for triplets, beams should only begin on downbeats, and beams should never cross from the "&" of 2 to beat 3."

If you would prefer to think of the rules stated this way, great! You will always produce clearly readable well-beamed notation. If you would prefer to think of the rules as we stated them above, "beams should never cross from the '&' of 2 to beat 3" is the equivalent of rule #1, and "Eighth notes in 4/4 should only be beamed in 4s or 2s to avoid them being mistaken for triplets, beams should only begin on downbeats" is the equivalent of combining rule #3 with a new rule #4 "Eighth notes should only be beamed in 4s and 2s."

Although everyone does not follow these more stringent rules, if you do, you will always produce well-beamed bars at the eighth note level in 4/4.

To be certain you understand these rules well, practice correcting the beaming of some poorly beamed examples. Take a poorly beamed example such as:

Example 1-058:

...and correct it. The above example, you notice, violates rule #1, which says to not beam between beats "2" and "3." When you correct this, you notice that you can also simplify this by using a staccato mark on a quarter note on beat "3" instead of an eighth note followed by an eighth rest. Your corrected version should look like:

Example 1-059:

Here is another poorly beamed example:

Example 1-060:

Notice that in Example 1-060, the second rule, which says to beam eighth notes that are part of the same beat, has been violated on beat "2" and on beat "4". The third rule, which says "do not beam between beats if neither of the beats themselves have beams"—or, as Arun would state it, "beams should only begin on downbeats" and "Eighth notes in 4/4 should only be beamed in 4s or 2s"—has been violated in the second half of the example.

So, a well-beamed notation of Example 1-060 would look like:

Example 1-061:

 You can practice correcting poorly beamed examples on Worksheet 1-W-014.

Practice Eighth Note Figures in 2/4

Although most eighth note level music we typically read is in 4/4 rather than 2/4, let's spend a little time reading and notating 2/4 examples in order to get familiar with the figures. We will focus on examples in which the notation shows the notes are sustained, although we realize that if we clap these examples, there will not be a way for us to sustain the notes in our performance.

When we count off these examples, we can use this count off:

Example 1-062:

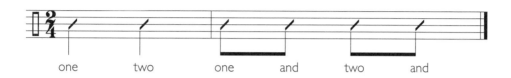

Note: other count offs are possible in 2/4. For example:

Example 1-063:

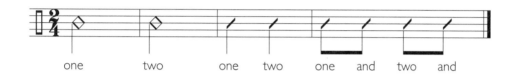

Practice reading these exercises:

Exercise 1-060:

Exercise 1-061:

Exercise 1-062:

Exercise 1-063:

Exercise 1-064:

Exercise 1-065:

Exercise 1-066:

Exercise 1-067:

Here are a couple of exercises with ties:

Exercise 1-068:

Exercise 1-069:

Here are a couple exercises with pickups:

Exercise 1-070:

Exercise 1-071:

 Here are some eighth note examples in 2/4 to transcribe for practice. Use Worksheet I-W-015.

Eighth Note Level from 2/4 to 4/4

We have spent some time with eighth note level figures in 2/4, even though our main interest for now is 4/4. Why? Because of this key point in writing eighth note level music in 4/4, each bar should contain two of the figures in 2/4 we have just examined.

This is a very important idea. NOTHING we write in 4/4 should look any different than the 2/4 figures we have already reviewed — the only difference in 4/4 is that there will be two of these figures in each bar.

We know these two figures in 2/4:

Example 1-064:

In a bar of 4/4 they will look like this:

Example 1-065:

Here are three different (but equivalent) ways of thinking about eighth note notation in 4/4. In each bar of 4/4:

• We can only combine two of the 2/4 figures we have already learned;
• We should be able to draw an imaginary bar line that separates the first 2 beats from the second 2 beats;
• We must show the "required beats" in each bar which, at the eighth note level, are beats "one" and "three;" and not unnecessarily show any other beats.

Practice converting eighth note music written in 2/4 by combining the bars into 4/4, making sure that you have followed these principles, using Worksheet 1-W-016.

It helps to practice correcting some poorly notated examples so you are certain you understand and can apply these notation principles. In the next section we will practice doing that.

Required Beats: Tips for Writing and Reading
A Bit More About Required Beats

We want to avoid two things: failing to show the required beats ("one" and "three") and showing any other beats unnecessarily.

Here is an example of failing to show a required beat (beat "three"). Notice that it does NOT look like two of the eighth note figures we have learned:

Example 1-066:

…and here is how it looks when corrected:

Example 1-067:

 Correct the examples of poorly notated music that fail to show required beats in Worksheet 1-W-017 and Worksheet 1-W-018.

The other mistake we want to avoid is writing things in a way where we are unnecessarily showing unrequired beats. Here is a poorly notated example in which that mistake is made:

Example 1-068:

…and a version that has been corrected:

Example 1-069:

 Correct the examples of poorly notated music that unnecessarily show unrequired beats on Worksheet 1-W-019.

Be sure that, while correcting one mistake, you do not introduce the other! There are a few more details about good notation discussed later on. But first, let's read through some eighth note music in 4/4.

The count off in 4/4 should be the same one we learned before:

Example 1-070:

Here is an exercise of some well notated eighth note level music in 4/4, combining some of the 2/4 figures we have looked at previously:

Exercise 1-072:

Do you find it more difficult to read these eighth note rhythms when they are written in 4/4? If so, here are four tips to make it easier.

Reading Tips for Eighth Notes in 4/4

First, review and be sure that the individual figures in 2/4 are all very easy for you to read and sing.

Second, try to make your eye look at two beats at a time, reading as though there were imaginary bar lines dividing each measure. If you do this successfully, it will be exactly as though you were reading the music in 2/4.

Third, try reading at a very slow tempo before you try a faster tempo, and feel the eighth notes even as you say the count off.

Fourth, if you need to, first translate this music to quarter note level music that sounds the same but is half as fast and see how that sounds. If you have gotten very confident with quarter note rhythms from our earlier exercises, this should help. To give an example of this, in Exercise 1-073, we have converted Exercise 1-072 to quarter note level. Sing Exercise 1-073, then go back and sing Exercise 1-072 again:

Exercise 1-073:

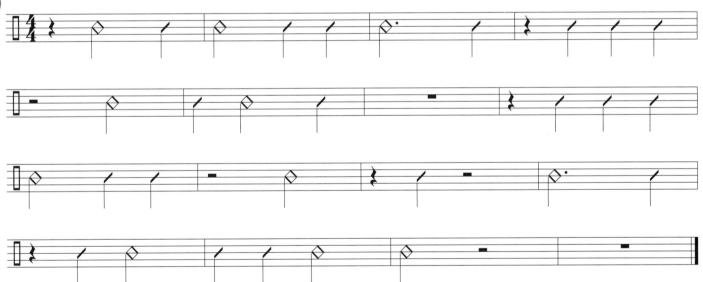

One more tip, especially for singers and wind players: when you are playing an eighth note on an "and" (i.e. on an off-beat) followed by a quarter rest or longer rest, be aware to correctly count the rest immediately following the eighth note. At first, a wind player or vocalist may find that rest feels "swallowed" by the eighth note, and have difficulty keeping track of it (guitarists, pianists, bassists and drummers can at least count the beat out loud). With experience, this becomes easy.
(Thanks to Dan Greenblatt for this observation!)

Swing Eighth Notes

I want to point out a choice in how to perform eighth notes. So far, we have been assuming they are performed "straight," which means they divide each beat evenly, and sound just like quarter notes would if the quarter notes were played twice as fast. But, there is another way to play them, which is with "swing feel."

Although there are many things that could be said about the feel of "swing eighth notes," for now we do not have to analyze them—just notice how they feel. (To discuss this in more depth, we need some more foundation, discussed in *THE RHYTHM BOOK—Intermediate Notation and Sight-Reading.*)

Listen to this example (on the book's website) played with a straight eighth note feel:

Example 1-071:

Straight Eighth Feel

… and how it would be played with swing eighth note feel:

Example 1-072:

Swing Eighth Feel

Exercises

Now that we know the full vocabulary of eighth note figures and most of what we need to best notate them in 4/4 (there are still a few notation refinements we will discuss), we need to practice reading and writing them.

We can practice at different tempos. Naturally, we will start off with tempos that we find easy (for most people, that means slower tempos—although extremely slow tempos can also be difficult). As you improve, you can gradually build up to practicing at faster tempos.

Play some of these examples with swing feel and others with straight eighth note feel.

Finally, as we have done from the beginning, you can continue to vary how you practice them: sing the rhythms while you clap either "one, two, three, four" or only on "one" and "three" or only on "two" and "four." Clap the rhythms instead of singing them while walking or tapping your foot at different rates (for example, while walking quarter notes, or while walking eighth notes); and do different combinations, such as walking quarter notes, and clapping on "2" and "4" while you sing the rhythms. Between all of these possibilities, as well as the choice of different tempos and straight eighth or swing feel, there are many variations in how you can practice each exercise.

We'll begin with some short exercises:

Exercise 1-074:

Exercise 1-075:

Exercise 1-076:

Exercise 1-077:

Exercise 1-078:

Exercise 1-079:

Exercise 1-080:

"On the Beat" VS "Off the Beat"

It is especially important to very clearly feel the distinction between notes that are "on the beat" and "off the beat":

On the beat:

Exercise 1-081:

...versus this (off the beat):

Exercise 1-082:

...and to be able to hear when the rhythm shifts from notes that are off the beat to notes that are on (or vice versa):

Exercise 1-083:

Eighth Note Exercises with Pickups

Here are some exercises with pickups:

Exercise 1-084:

Exercise 1-085:

Exercise 1-086:

Exercise 1-087:

Exercise 1-088:

Exercise 1-089:

Exercise 1-090:

Exercise 1-091:

Eighth Note Exercises with Ties

Here are some exercises with ties (notice that our examples are getting longer—if these are too long for you at first, concentrate on just correctly reading one or two bars at a time, but continue to work at correctly reading longer examples without stopping):

Exercise 1-092:

Exercise 1-093:

Exercise 1-094:

Exercise 1-095:

Exercise 1-096:

Exercise 1-097:

Exercise 1-098:

Exercise 1-099:

Eighth Note Exercises with Pickups and Ties

The following exercises use both ties and pickups:

Exercise 1-100:

Exercise 1-101:

Exercise 1-102:

Exercise 1-103:

Notice that in the following exercise, the last two notes at the end of the last bar sounds like a pickup the second time when you perform the bars within the repeat signs, but it is a different figure than the pickup at the beginning of the exercise:

Exercise 1-104:

Notice that in Exercise 1-105, the last two notes of the last measure feel like a pickup when you take the repeat, but like a different pickup than the initial one.

Exercise 1-105:

Exercise 1-106:

Exercise 1-107:

Gradually, you will want to work on reading, writing, and transcribing longer exercises.
Begin with the short transcriptions, then proceed to the longer ones.
Short exercises to begin: Worksheet 1-W-020
Exercises with pickups: Worksheet 1-W-021
Exercises with ties: Worksheet 1-W-022
Longer exercises, with ties: Worksheet 1-W-023
Longer exercises, with pickups and ties: Worksheet 1-W-024
Before we practice more exercises, let's first examine the staccato mark, and its use in simplifying notation.

Phrasing
The Staccato Mark

Articulation marks are used to provide more detail about how the written notes should be performed. A thorough review of articulation marks is provided in *THE RHYTHM BOOK—Intermediate Notation and Sight-Reading*, but for now there is one, the **staccato mark**, of special importance to us because it can be used to simplify rhythmic notation and make it easier for others to read.

The staccato mark is a dot written immediately below or above the head of a note. If the note is written with stem up, we place the staccato mark immediately below the note head; if it's written stem down, the staccato mark is placed immediately above it.

Example 1-073:

Staccato means "detached"—so if a staccato note is followed by another note, the staccato note is not sustained directly into the following note—there is some silence between the notes. Thus, the staccato mark tells us to play a note "short"—do not sustain the sound for the entire written duration of the note. For example, instead of:

Example 1-074:

...you can use staccato marks and write:

Example 1-075:

...which will sound the same.

If we use staccato in an example with pitches, the staccato marks will usually be written so that they are consistently on the opposite side of the note head from it's stem, even if the stem direction changes within the measure.

So, instead of this:

Example 1-076:

…we could write this:

Example 1-077:

The examples we've looked at so far have notes that fall on the beats and are not sustained; this is a clear case where the version with staccato marks has fewer things written in the bar and is easier to read. Can we also use staccato marks for notes that fall off beats? Yes, as the following examples reveal.

Instead of this:

Example 1-078:

… we could write this:

Example 1-079:

Let's pause for a moment to reconsider the idea of shorter vs. longer note durations in an example. We know that, in the following two examples, we will sing notes on the same beats, that some of the notes will be made shorter in the first example and sustained longer in the second example, and that the first example can be a bit more difficult to read because there are more things in each bar:

Example 1-080:

Example 1-081:

We want to be comfortable notating things either way, and converting between one and the other (as we did in the previous two examples). You can practice this conversion using Worksheet 1-W-025.

Now, let's consider in a bit more depth the use of staccato. Classical musicians have several different articulation symbols that describe making a note shorter to different degrees. They tend to look at these degrees in great detail—which seems appropriate to a music whose focus is exquisite performance of written music previously composed by someone else. Some speak of the staccato mark as reducing the sustain of any note by one half of its value. Others disagree. So, some would agree with my statement that Example 1-074 and Example 1-075 sound the same, and others would disagree. But for our purposes, with regard to jazz and contemporary music, we want to consider two things: 1) common practice and 2) appropriate level of precision.

For some instruments, staccato is associated with a particular technique (e.g. tonguing by horn players), but readers are to understand it is not being used that way here.

Most rhythmic notation principles are quite consistent and logical, but common practice in the use of staccato is a bit different. For example, it would logically make sense that we could write whole notes or half notes with staccato marks but, in the context of jazz, these are almost never seen. It would make sense that, if we wanted to play this phrase:

Example 1-082:

but making the notes shorter, we could write it like this:

Example 1-083:

…. in fact, on occasion, I myself have broken with common practice and done exactly that—it just seems so logical and clear. But the common practice is not to put staccato marks on dotted notes and in polling many colleagues who are expert and experienced readers, I find they insist that they would prefer to see the above example following common practice as this:

Example 1-084:

So, of the types of notes we've learned so far, staccato marks are used commonly only with the quarter notes and eighth notes. For now, we will not concern ourselves with staccato eighth notes. But, we can summarize that, when possible, short notes that fall on beats are very commonly written as quarter notes with staccato marks; and short notes that fall on the "and" of beat one and the "and" of beat three sometimes are written as quarter notes with staccato marks.

The reason staccato marks can help so much in simplifying notation is that, especially in the frequent cases where we do not care about being extremely precise about how long notes are sustained, they allow us to write less on the page. We can make the examples sound like the "short duration" versions without writing all the rests. This is more easy on the eyes of the readers (less clutter).

Compare these two examples, which illustrate this:

Example 1-085:

Example 1-086:

…and notice how much less there is in the second example for your eye to take in.

53

Since our goal is to make rhythms as clear and easy to read as possible, you can see how the staccato mark is a powerful tool to use towards this goal. Here is another example—compare these two versions, and notice how much easier it is to read the one that uses staccato marks:

Example 1-087:

… than it is to read the version that instead writes out all the rests:

Example 1-088:

 Practice using the staccato mark to convert examples on Worksheet 1-W-026.

It is not "wrong" to write with rests instead of staccato marks—it's just that the staccato mark can help produce a version that is preferable. Would there ever be a situation in which writing the precise duration of a short note would be better than using the staccato mark? Yes, there are two that come to mind: 1) A piece that is at a very slow tempo, performed by instruments that sustain notes (e.g. a choir of voices or a violin section), in which we want all the instruments to sustain the notes and end them together in a very precise way (this would probably involve using shorter note values—16th notes or even 32nd notes—that we have not yet discussed); or 2) A situation (e.g. sight-reading by a big band) in which we don't "trust" the musicians to notice the staccato marks on the first read-through, and want to be certain they play the notes short.

However, in general, I find that it is more common for people to under-use rather than overuse the power of the staccato mark in simplifying notation. While the staccato mark is the articulation that will most commonly help in simplifying notation, we can state this general principle about good notation: Use articulation marks to simplify notation when possible.

Interpretation of Quarter Notes in Eighth Note Music

We should consider a question of interpretation. We have just discussed the use of the staccato mark to indicate that a quarter note should be played shorter (not sustained for its full duration). But, in some styles of music, the conventional interpretation is to make quarter notes shorter even if no staccato marks are used in the notation. For example, if given the following example in a chart played with a medium swing feel, experienced sight-readers would typically play the first three notes in the first bar and the first note in the second bar as short:

Example 1-089:

This example is courtesy of Dan Greenblatt, who might describe it syllable-wise in swing feel as "boop boop boop ba doop doo."

The same written music, if played in certain Afro-Cuban styles, would tend to be interpreted with those notes more sustained. So, one must be aware of the conventions of the musical style in which one is playing, not only depending on articulation (such as staccato) marks, when it comes to interpreting quarter notes.

Appropriate Precision in Rhythmic Notation

When we previously discussed the staccato mark, the first of the two situations we mentioned in which one might not choose to use it is where extreme precision of note duration is needed. Let's further discuss appropriate precision in rhythmic notation.

There are two ways we can go wrong with respect to precision: too little (which can involve either inaccuracies or not being sufficiently specific, for example, about note duration, phrasing, etc.) or too much.

If you write something with too little precision, here is a way it may prove obvious to you: give it to other musicians, without singing or playing it for them (which could allow them to correct your mistakes, whether consciously or unconsciously) and have them perform what you have written. Does it sound as you wanted it to? If so, it is a good indication you have been sufficiently precise. If not, perhaps you suspect they are not reading it correctly. However, if you give it to other musicians and none of them play it so that it sounds the way you want, you should question whether you have written it sufficiently precisely and clearly.

Less obvious is the opposite problem: you have written it too precisely. In this case, when it is performed it will likely sound as you want it to. So, is there any problem with being overly precise? Surprisingly, the answer is "yes." Almost always, an overly precise notation is more difficult to read. At times, it is so difficult to read that musicians have trouble performing it correctly; but, in many cases, although they manage to play it so it sounds right, it makes them work much harder than necessary.

> As a general rule, we want to rhythmically notate in the way that is most simple and easy to read, while still producing the desired sound. Being overly precise gets in the way of this, and makes things more difficult to read. In *THE RHYTHM BOOK—Intermediate Notation and Sight-Reading*, I show you examples of the mistakes people make in being overly precise, but they involve notation we haven't yet examined.

For now, we can formulate one more principle of good rhythmic notation: write rhythms with the appropriate degree of precision. They should be as easy to read as possible and as precise as necessary (but not more so).

Use Worksheet I-W-027 to practice correcting poorly notated examples, and indicate the notation principle(s) that were violated in each case.

Eighth Notes, Continued
Longer and Two-Part Exercises
Longer Eighth Note Exercises
Now, we can practice some longer eighth note exercises.

First, let me explain first and second endings. In this example, play the first three bars and go to the first ending. Then, play everything again from the repeat sign, but this time, skip to the the second ending. So, when you read this:

Example 1-090:

… you should actually play this:

Example 1-091:

Read these exercises:

Exercise 1-108:

Exercise 1-109:

Exercise 1-110:

Here is an exercise based on the blues form, that uses space:

Exercise 1-111:

Exercise 1-112:

(this exercise continues on next page)

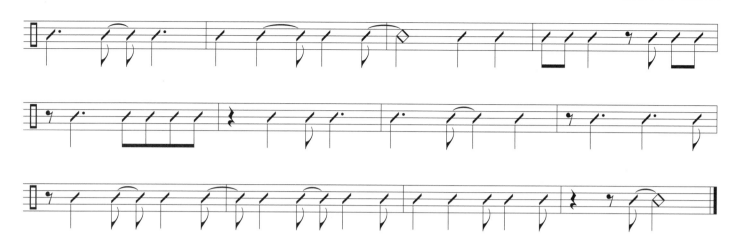

In this exercise, I attempted to write some rhythms similar to what a drummer might play on his or her snare drum while playing accompaniment in swing:

 Exercise 1-113:

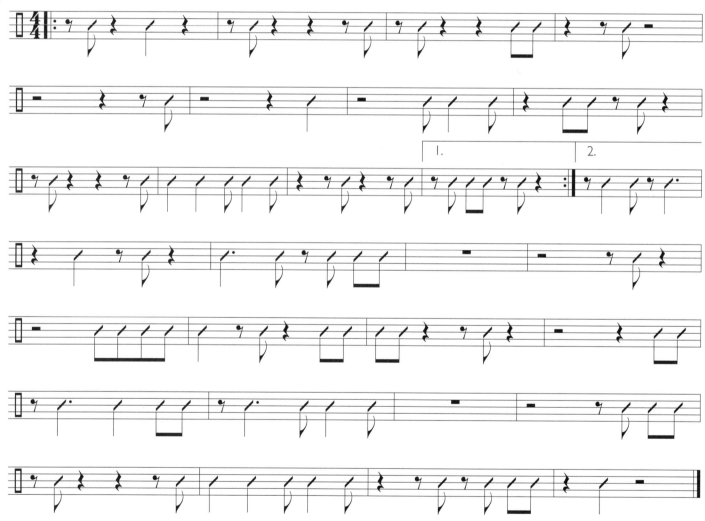

...and one more (notice that, unlike other exercises, which are in four and eight bar phrases, the first section of this one is in ten bar phrases. That's just what feels right to me in this exercise):

Exercise 1-114:

 Try transcribing the longer eighth note level example on Worksheet 1-W-028. If you have to transcribe a bar or two at a time, that's fine: this is intended to help prepare you for transcribing heads (melodies of tunes) and solos.

Eighth Note Exercises in Two Parts

Once you have gotten very strong at reading the eighth note exercises, one way to increase the challenge is to read studies that have multiple parts. The exercises here have two parts to be performed simultaneously. You can do these whether you have one other person or an entire group with whom to practice. Choose who will read each part, count off the exercise, and begin together. The added challenge in this comes in your being strong at correctly reading your part while you hear the "distraction" of another part being sung simultaneously. At first, you may need to concentrate a lot on your own part and on the beat and not focus on what your partner is singing (perhaps almost ignoring them if you find you are really struggling). As you gain confidence, you can listen more to your partner. These exercises also put a premium on your keeping in the right place at all costs (even if you sing something incorrectly in one bar, you must start the next bar at the right time to stay synchronized with the other part). Exercise 1-115 can be performed with either straight or swing eighth note feel:

Exercise 1-115:

The first part of this exercise is based on the blues. Sing it with swing eighth note feel:

Exercise 1-116:

This is a two-part eighth note funk study. Start by singing it with straight eighth note feel. Some shuffle-funk or hip-hop-style funk actually has swing eighth notes, so you can read through it a second time, swinging the eighth notes:

Exercise 1-117:

Try transcribing these two-part eighth note level examples: Worksheet 1-W-029.
Try singing each part in this example: Worksheet 1-W-030.
Try Group Exercises: Worksheet 1-W-031.

Exercises with Pitches
Sight-Reading Rhythms on Your Instrument

If you have gone through the exercises and worksheets, by now you are acquiring some mastery of sight-reading and writing rhythms. You have worked on performance variations with singing rhythms and clapping rhythms along with conveying pulse by walking, foot tapping, finger snapping, clapping, hand tapping, counting, or simply feeling the pulse internally. Now, it is time to work on sight-reading on your instrument. Please notice I have intentionally had you work on all of these variations away from your instrument first.

In a sense, there are no additional skills needed to read on your instrument. Yet, I find that, for some students, their reading of rhythms on their instrument is initially not at as high a level. Here are some suggestions.

First, practice reading exercises written in rhythmic notation, like those you have been reading up until now in this book but, instead of singing, tapping, or clapping them, play them using one repeated note on your instrument. This will be a bit different from instrument to instrument. If you are a pianist, it will be just pushing down one key, somewhat similar to tapping the rhythm. Similarly, drummers and vibes players can use sticks or mallets, respectively to "tap" the rhythm on one drum or bar of the vibes. Guitarists just pick one note repeatedly. Other string players (bassists, cellists, violists, violinists) repeatedly play the rhythm with one pizzicato note. Notice that, even with the instruments we have mentioned, there are some decisions you have to make; I have not spelled out everything. For example, for the pianists and string players, should all the notes be played or plucked by one finger or alternating between two or more fingers? At very fast tempi, the tempo may dictate the choice but, in general, I recommend that you try the different possibilities and see what works best for you. Similarly for guitarists, who must choose whether to pick with all upstrokes, all downstrokes, or strictly alternate picking direction (or other possibilities, such as downstrokes for all notes that are on beats and upstrokes for all notes off beats), and drummers and vibists, who must choose sticking patterns. Wind and brass players play one repeating note; to add interest, if you can, you might try using an "alternate" or "false" fingering, and switch between two ways of producing the same note. For singers, there is little new in this exercise, except producing a beautiful vocal note rather than a spoken "dah."

While you read the rhythms by playing them on the instrument, try some of the foot tapping possibilities we discussed: tapping on "2" and "4," or on "1" and "3," on "1," "2," "3," "4," on just "1," and on just "3," as well as playing them without tapping. Try this tapping with either foot or doing things in combinations ("1," "2," "3," "4," alternating between feet—so, for example, tap "1" and "3" with your right foot, and "2" and "4" with your left foot). If you are a drummer, you could choose to do any of this by tapping on bass drum and/or hi hat pedals.

Go back and read through a number of the exercises in this book, playing them on your instrument repeating one note. When that is quite easy, make up other variations for fun. For example, alternate between two pitches; play the rhythms with notes of scales or arpeggios or other note sequences, and find other variations you enjoy.

The next step on your instrument will be reading exercises in normal (not rhythmic) notation where pitches are specified.

Sight-Reading Pitches

Unless you play unpitched percussion instruments, such as woodblock, cowbell, or claves, most of your real-world experience in reading rhythms will be with music in standard notation where you must simultaneously read both pitches and rhythms. Yet we have intentionally avoided pitches until now, as there is great value to putting focus on one element (just the rhythms) to improve most rapidly in that area. I am confident that, even without this section, the reader who has thoroughly mastered the material so far will find it a fairly smooth transition to reading standard notation. However, let's introduce some exercises for practice.

My suggestion is that you first try reading some of these away from your instrument, singing the pitches. When that is comfortable, sight read them on your instrument, playing the written pitches. If you have any trouble making the transition to reading standard notation music that combines both rhythms and pitches, there is something you can do even before singing the pitches away from your instrument. First read only the rhythms and, only then, begin to read the pitches. To simulate this, we will read an exercise in rhythmic notation:

Exercise 1-118:

...then a rhythmically identical exercise in standard notation:

Exercise 1-119:

Of course, typically, you would only receive the standard notation version of the chart, but you could consciously ignore the pitches at first while you read the rhythms. Try doing this with the following exercise. The first time, read just its rhythms; the second time, read the pitches as well.

Exercise 1-120:

66

Multi-Part Exercises with Pitches

In these multi-part exercises with pitches, you can assign one part to a friend (or fellow student, if you are using this book in a class), and the other to yourself. If you are doing the exercise by yourself, do it with a recording in which the other part is played.

This exercise is based on a blues. Play it with swing eighth note feel:

Exercise 1-121:

Here is an exercise to be played with straight eighth note feel (bossa nova):

Exercise 1-122:

Harmonically, this exercise is based on the first section of a standard tune. Notice rhythmically in these multi-part exercises you must be strong on your part, which at times is rhythmically "against" the other part, and at times lines up with it. Play this with swing eighth feel:

Exercise 1-123:

Finally, here is a 3-part exercise with pitches, to be played with straight eighth note feel. There is a lot going on here; make sure to not let the other parts sway you from the rhythmic integrity and accuracy of your part:

 Exercise 1-124:

(1st x only)

Here is a version of Exercise 1-116, which we read previously, but with pitches added:

Exercise 1-125:

Here is Exercise 1-117 but with pitches:

Exercise 1-126:

Triplet Eighth Notes
Introduction to Triplet Eighths

We have looked at the rhythms we can construct with whole notes, half notes, quarter notes, and eighth notes. All of these are sometimes called duple divisions: they divide by two (so, a quarter note lasts half as long as a half note, an eighth note last half as long as a quarter, etc.). Now let's look at an example of a triple division: **triplet eighth notes**. If you take a quarter note and divide it into three equal parts, these will be triplet eighth notes. A bar of 4/4 filled with triplet eighth notes will look like this:

Example 1-092:

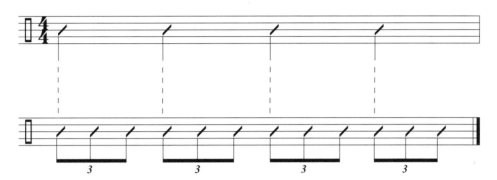

To be certain you are playing them accurately, you can practice them at first alternating with quarter notes, to be certain your pulse is steady:

Exercise 1-127:

Notice that the number "3" written below the three eighth notes is all you need to write to indicate these are triplets. But let's consider for a moment what the "3" really means. We are dividing a quarter note into three equal parts, writing three eighth notes (which would normally take one and a half beats), but the number "3" tells us to "squeeze" them, to fit three of them in the time it would normally take to play two eighth notes. Although we will only look at triplet eighth notes for now, any time you see a "3" written over some notes, it means to squeeze in this "three in the time of two" way.

We know that, for quarter note level music in 4/4, the required beat to show is "one"; and that, for eighth note level music in 4/4, the required beats to show are "one" and "three." What about for music that is at the triplet eighth note level? Once we have "broken triplets" (discussed in the following section) and syncopated figures at the triplet eighth note level, we will want to show every beat ("one," "two," "three," and "four"). But if we are just putting a beat's worth of triplet eighth notes on one or two of the beats, it is fine to simply show "one" and "three." So, for example, rather than this:

Example 1-093:

…it would be fine to write this:

Example 1-094:

Try transcribing these eighth note level examples with triplets: Worksheet 1-W-032.

Broken Triplets

Just as you can use ties when playing quarter notes or eighth notes, you can tie triplets. This allows for these two possibilities:

Example 1-095:

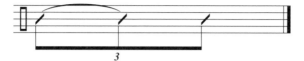

Example 1-096:

But, this is not the preferred way to notate them. Even if you show "one," "two," "three," and "four" with triplet eighth notes, you do not have to show every triplet eighth. Showing every beat is plenty!

Therefore, instead of this:

write this:

Example 1-097:

...and, instead of this:

write this:

Example 1-098:

Also like quarter notes and eighth notes, we have the possibility of tying together triplet eighth notes. Sometimes, the term "broken triplets" is used to distinguish from a constant stream of triplets. If we use many ties with the two new figures we are looking at, we can produce syncopated rhythms of "broken triplets" that can be somewhat challenging to read. Here is an example of these syncopated "broken triplets" using ties:

Example 1-099:

Exercises
Triplet Eighth Note Exercises

Although I have made you aware of tricky "broken triplet" rhythms that are possible, for now our goal is just to be able to recognize and to sing triplets in the context of an eighth note exercise.

Sing the following exercise, being certain that the triplet evenly divides its beat into three equal parts.

Try this exercise sung with straight eighth note feel, and then with swing feel:

Exercise 1-128:

Although you can also try this with straight eighth note feel, it and many of the exercises that follow are conceived with swing feel in mind:

Exercise 1-129:

With this exercise, there are no eighth notes, so it does not matter whether you think "straight eighth feel" or "swing eighth feel."

Exercise 1-130:

 Practice hearing and notating more short examples with triplet eighth notes using Worksheet 1-W-033. Now, we introduce some exercises with pickups and triplet eighth notes. These are swing eighth feel:

Exercise 1-131:

Triplets can be in the pickup itself ...:

Exercise 1-132:

Play these with the repeats:

 Exercise 1-133:

 Exercise 1-134:

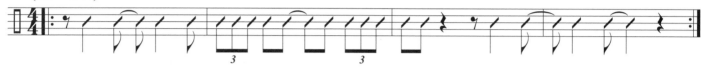

Feel all three triplet eighth notes on the last beat, but only sing the last two:

 Exercise 1-135:

 Transcribe triplet eighth note examples with pickups using Worksheet I-W-034.

Triplet Eighth Note Exercises with Pitches

Next, we introduce some exercises with triplet eighth notes that include pitches. If necessary, ignore the pitches the first time you read any that you find difficult, then sing the pitches the second time. If you find that you can read the pitches as well right from the first time, that is great!

Exercise 1-136:

Although you may be able to sing it faster, this exercise was conceived as being played at a very relaxed medium-slow tempo:

Exercise 1-137:

Here's another exercise conceived as no faster than medium tempo, with swing eighth note feel:

Exercise 1-138:

Try this one somewhat faster. It can be felt as straight eighth or swing:

Exercise 1-139:

Swing eighth note feel on the next two exercises:

Exercise 1-140:

Make sure that the B and G♯ at the end of the exercise sound like the first two notes of a triplet, but with the G♯ subsequently sustained:

Exercise 1-141:

Here is a two-part exercise with triplet eighth notes and swing eighth note feel. In the first version, read only the rhythms:

Exercise 1-142:

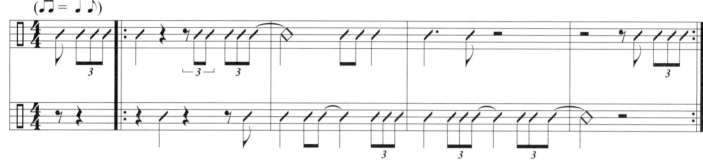

…but now, read the same thing but with pitches:

Exercise 1-143:

In *THE RHYTHM BOOK—Intermediate Notation and Sight-Reading*, we explore more about triplets: triplet quarter notes, triplet half notes, triplet sixteenth notes, and syncopated figures with broken triplets. For now, if you can read and write the kinds of exercises we have just examined, that's terrific. If these still prove difficult, create more examples of your own using triplet eighth notes.

Feel Divisions of the Beat

Now that we have introduced different rates of notes: quarter note level, eighth note level, and triplet eighth note level, there is one more step you should employ when you transcribe a rhythmic example: confirm that you are at the correct rhythmic level. Whether the example is a recording in a familiar style, or someone counting off and playing or singing an example, notice how fast the beat is, and create "grids," testing which "grid" the example falls on. For example, tap each quarter note while you sing the rhythm and notice if you are singing anything that does not fall on one of the beats you are tapping. If not, your example is at quarter note level. If so, try tapping every eighth note while you sing the example; etc.

In the case of music in a familiar style—for example, 4/4 swing with bass walking quarter notes; or "two-feel" with bass largely playing half notes, plus some connecting phrases; or syncopated funk—it is easy to know what the pulse is by knowing the style (example: walking 4/4, so the bass is playing quarter notes). In the case of a musical example with a count-off, pay careful attention to the count-off itself to identify the pulse.

Of course, the rate of notes—the "grid" on which the music lies—could change from measure to measure, or even from beat to beat. However, if you practice transcribing rhythms, you will easily notice and be able to feel such a change in rate. By far the more common problem I see is that of mistakenly thinking the rate of notes change in the middle of a phrase when it does not. We examine this further and look at examples in *THE RHYTHM BOOK—Intermediate Notation and Sight-Reading*.

Conclusions

As we conclude this book, I want to encourage you to review and spend more time with any material we have covered that is still tricky for you. Once you have mastered everything here, you will see it will serve as an excellent solid foundation for all the more advanced rhythmic notation material in *THE RHYTHM BOOK—Intermediate Notation and Sight-Reading.*

The command you develop in reading and writing rhythms will enable you to communicate rhythmic material easily. This will serve you well, whether in reading music written by others, writing your own charts, or understanding and learning the rhythmic concepts and practices described in other books in this collection.

Congratulations on working through the material in this book!

Appendices
Appendix 1: Performance Variations
Simple Variations
Here are performance variations in which we never do more than one rhythm with the feet and one rhythm with the hands:

Voice	Hands	Feet
say "1 2 3 4"	clap or tap rhythm	(none)
say "1 2 3 4"	clap or tap rhythm	walk quarter notes
say "1 2 3 4"	clap or tap rhythm	tap "1"
say "1 2 3 4"	clap or tap rhythm	tap "1" and "3"
say "1 2 3 4"	clap or tap rhythm	tap "2" and "4"
(none)	clap or tap rhythm	walk quarter notes
(none)	clap or tap rhythm	tap "1"
(none)	clap or tap rhythm	tap "1" and "3"
(none)	clap or tap rhythm	tap "2" and "4"
sing rhythm	clap or tap quarter notes	(none)
sing rhythm	clap or tap "1"	(none)
sing rhythm	clap or tap "1" and "3"	(none)
sing rhythm	clap or tap "2" and "4"	(none)
sing rhythm	clap or tap "3"	(none)
sing rhythm	clap or tap "1"	walk quarter notes
sing rhythm	clap or tap "1" and "3"	walk quarter notes
sing rhythm	clap or tap "2" and "4"	walk quarter notes
sing rhythm	clap or tap "3"	walk quarter notes
sing rhythm	clap or tap "1"	tap quarter notes
sing rhythm	clap or tap "1"	tap "1" and "3"
sing rhythm	clap or tap "1"	tap "2" and "4"
sing rhythm	clap or tap "2"	tap "1"
sing rhythm	clap or tap "3"	tap "1"
sing rhythm	clap or tap "1"	tap "3"
sing rhythm	clap or tap "1"	tap "2" and "4"
sing rhythm	snap fingers on quarter notes	(none)
sing rhythm	snap fingers on "1"	(none)
sing rhythm	snap fingers on "1" and "3"	(none)
sing rhythm	snap fingers on "2" and "4"	(none)
sing rhythm	snap fingers on "3"	(none)
sing rhythm	snap fingers on "1"	walk quarter notes
sing rhythm	snap fingers on "1" and "3"	walk quarter notes
sing rhythm	snap fingers on "2" and "4"	walk quarter notes
sing rhythm	snap fingers on "3"	walk quarter notes
sing rhythm	snap fingers on "1"	tap quarter notes
sing rhythm	snap fingers on "1"	tap "1" and "3"
sing rhythm	snap fingers on "1"	tap "2" and "4"
sing rhythm	snap fingers on "2"	tap "1"
sing rhythm	snap fingers on "3"	tap "1"
sing rhythm	snap fingers on "1"	tap "3"
sing rhythm	snap fingers on "1"	tap "2" and "4"

Variations with Hand and Feet Independence

Here are a few performance variations with different things in the two hands and/or feet - you can make up more of these:

Voice	Left Hand	Right Hand	Left Foot	Right Foot
(none)	tap "2" and "4"	tap rhythm	tap "1"	(none)
(none)	snap "2" and "4"	tap rhythm	(none)	tap "1"
(none)	tap rhythm	tap "2" and "4"	tap "1"	(none)
(none)	tap rhythm	tap "1" and "3"	(none)	(none)
sing rhythm	tap "2" and "4"	tap "1"	(none)	(none)
sing rhythm	tap "2" and "4"	(none)	(none)	tap "1"
sing rhythm	snap "1"	(none)	tap "2" and "4"	tap "1" and "3"

Make up additional variations of your own!

Incorporating Foot Tapping While Playing Instrument

Depending on what instrument you play, if your feet are available (you aren't a drummer, pianist using the sustain pedal, organ player playing pedals, etc.) try different variations of foot tapping (none; one foot on "2" and "4;" one foot on "2" and "4" while the other is on "1;" one foot on "1" and "3;" etc.)

Appendix II: Practice with Recordings and with Others

Two essential skills to develop are the abilities to hear rhythms in the context of song forms and to hear multiple simultaneous parts. Both of these skills are important in jazz, Brazilian, Afro-Cuban, funk, and the wide variety of other music that developed when African rhythms came to the New World.

Although this book focuses on the basics of rhythmic notation and sight-reading, it is useful for a student of music to begin to develop skills at hearing song form and multiple simultaneous parts as early as possible. Thus, we introduce work with pre-recorded group exercises early in the text (Worksheet 1-W-009, Worksheet 1-W-010 and Worksheet 1-W-011; and again with Worksheet 1-W-031). In this appendix, we will briefly look at how to do group exercises live and how to create your own group exercises, as well as how to practice with recordings.

Practice with Others

In order to do a group exercise live, a teacher, or one member of a group who acts as leader can create and teach parts to others. Although these parts can be planned in advance, I prefer in keeping with the improvisational spirit of the music to create them on the spot. Depending on the number of participants, each person can be given an individual rhythm part, or participants can be divided into sub-groups, each of which is given one part.

The leader starts with a countoff and some method to keep the pulse—perhaps clapping on "two" and "four" or foot tapping—and sings the first part to the person or sub-group responsible for it. The leader repeats the part in time and, as soon as possible, those responsible for that part sing it along with the leader. As they continue to sing their part, the leader begins singing a different part for the next participant(s). One by one, parts are added, until there are several parts being sung at once. The leader can signal for some parts to be sung more softly while one part is sung more loudly, in order to be certain everyone can hear that part. The goal for each participant is to accurately sing his or her part while hearing as many of the other parts as possible.

As all the parts are being performed, the leader can count quarter notes to be certain all the participants know and remember where their parts fit in the time. For example, for a two-bar repeating pattern in 4/4, the leader would count "ONE, two, three, four, TWO, two, three, four." Then, the leader signals everyone to stop. After a moment's pause, the leader counts off at the same tempo, and participants must come in singing their parts in the correct place in time. When this has been done successfully, the leader signals everyone to stop again, but this time counts off at a slower or faster tempo. This is done several times until everyone can correctly come in on their parts at a wide variety of tempos (including quite fast and slow).

Next, the leader directs each participant to switch to singing a part previously sung by someone else. If participants have succeeded at hearing and remembering all of the parts, they can make this switch correctly the first time. If not, everyone can be instructed to return to singing their original parts so that each participant can listen again and focus on the part to which he or she will have to switch.

The leader should choose rhythms appropriate to what is being studied by participants. For those working through this book, the parts might start out being based on quarter notes. A few weeks later, group exercises could be based on eighth notes, and subsequently, on triplet eighths. The individual parts should, in the first weeks, be very short and simple. As the group studies the materials and makes progress, individual parts can be more challenging (e.g. more syncopated, or longer) in subsequent weeks.

I have described this as a group of people "singing" different parts, but variations can include different ways of playing parts through clapping, tapping, stomping, finger-snapping, speaking, or making different vocal sounds. These can be mixed, so that, for example, some are singing a bass part, some clapping, some making a mouth percussion sound, some singing a high melody line, and so forth.

It is helpful to build the physical connection to rhythm. A book in this collection, *THE RHYTHM BOOK – Rhythmic Development and Performance in 4/4*, describes a number of practices from around the world that can be used in making this connection. Even if you just perform parts while walking in place or tapping feet, clapping, and singing, you will build more physical connection to rhythms and grooves.

For additional notation practice, immediately after performing a group exercise, participants can be asked to notate their part, and as many other parts as they can remember. These transcribed parts can be compared for accuracy and adherence to principles of good notation.

This entire description of how to do group exercises is based on things that I have come up with, tried, and, as an instructor, found to work. Do not let this limit you; look for other ways to do group exercises that you invent or that you see other instructors use. For an online journal article I've written for teachers about these group exercises, please see Engaging Students Through Jazz: http://flipcamp.org/engagingstudents4/

Practice with Recordings

You can sight-read and perform any of the exercises in this book along with a recording. Choose a recording of a piece of music at an appropriate tempo, and play or sing the written exercise, repeating it as you listen to the recording playing behind you. Pay attention at each moment to what is happening in the recording, and where you are in the form, even as you make certain to play your rhythm accurately. Choose a way to mark the beginning of each section of the piece being performed on the recording (e.g. with a foot stomp). Work on playing or singing your rhythm so that it is very "locked in" with the recording, and grooving.

When you first begin to practice singing or clapping a rhythm along with a recording, you may find that a lot of your focus is on performing your part correctly, and you are using the recording mostly as though it were a metronome. As you get more comfortable performing your part, work on shifting your focus more and more to listening to the recording: to the details of chord voicings played by the pianist, rhythmic and pitch choices by the bassist, hits played by the drummer, lines played by horns and parts played by others. When you perform with others on your instrument, work on using these same listening skills.

As your rhythmic sight-reading improves and you get comfortable playing the exercises along with recordings, choose different recordings—some swinging, some straight eighth note, in different styles; and work some on playing with recordings at a faster tempo each week.

Appendix III: Exercises for Piano

Pianists have a unique set of opportunities when performing the rhythm exercises on their instrument. If you are a pianist, you would first want to be completely comfortable with performing an exercise away from your instrument, using several of the variations summarized in Appendix I. When you then perform the exercise on your instrument, there are many possibilities for how to do this.

For example, what can you do on your instrument after practicing Exercise 1-100 on page 49 away from it?

Here is Exercise 1-100 without pitches:

First, you could play it with just one hand, on a repeated note. With you right hand:

Exercise 1-144:

or with your left hand:

Exercise 1-145:

Next, you could play it in rhythmic unison with both hands on the same pitch:

Exercise 1-146:

or on different pitches:

Exercise 1-147:

Play it with one hand while playing on beat one with the other hand:

Exercise 1-148:

Exercise 1-149:

or on beats one and three with the other hand:

Exercise 1-150:

Exercise 1-151:

or on beats two and four with other hand:

Exercise 1-152:

Exercise 1-153:

Choose a groove to play with one hand, such as the "Charleston" (beats one and the and of two), while you play the exercise rhythm with the other hand:

Exercise 1-154:

Exercise 1-155:

Switch which hand plays the groove and which plays the exercise rhythm:

Exercise 1-156:

Next, you could choose pitches to play in the exercise rhythm:

Exercise 1-157:

Play this with both hands in octaves:

Exercise 1-158:

or harmonized, for example in 10ths:

Exercise 1-159:

Then play some of the variations we've just done, but using these pitches:

Exercise 1-160:

Exercise 1-161:

Exercise 1-162:

Exercise 1-163:

As you can see, there are many possibilities, and you can come up with more of your own. Of course, after a while, you get to know this exercise rhythm well and it is time to move on to other rhythms. You may find that doing a few of these variations with each exercise rhythm is plenty, but it is good to choose different variations each time; flexibility is a virtue!

Appendix IV: Exercises for Drums

Drummers are presented with many choices when they perform the rhythm exercises on their instrument. Like a pianist, a drummer should first be completely comfortable with performing an exercise away from the drums, using several of the variations summarized in Appendix I. When you perform the exercise on drums, here are some of the things you can do. Please note that I leave sticking patterns and variations for you.

For example, take Exercise 1-105 on page 49:

For these examples we will use this simple drum key:

Bass Drum	Low Tom	Snare Drum	High Tom	Ride Cymbal	Hi-hat Foot

Play this rhythm on snare drum alone:

 Exercise 1-164:

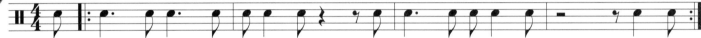

on bass drum alone:

 Exercise 1-165:

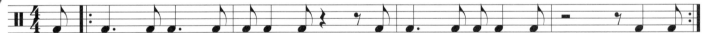

on ride cymbal alone:

 Exercise 1-166:

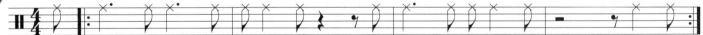

and on hi-hat alone:

 Exercise 1-167:

Play it simultaneously on combinations of these, such as ride cymbal and snare drum:

Exercise 1-168:

On your own, choose other combinations on which to play it simultaneously, such as snare drum and bass drum, or hi-hat and bass drum, or ride cymbal and hi-hat, or hi-hat and snare drum.

Play it between snare and low tom:

Exercise 1-169:

or between high tom and low tom:

Exercise 1-170:

or between high tom and bass drum:

Exercise 1-171:

Try passing the rhythm between limbs in different ways such as:

Exercise 1-172:

or:

Exercise 1-173:

Play quarter notes on the ride cymbal, while playing the rhythm on the snare:

 Exercise 1-174:

or while passing the rhythm between two drums as we did before, such as between high tom and bass drum:

 Exercise 1-175:

or between snare drum and low tom:

 Exercise 1-176:

With swing feel, add the rhythm to more conventional drum parts. For example, play quarter notes on the ride cymbal, with the hi-hat playing on "two" and "four," adding the rhythm on the snare drum:

 Exercise 1-177:

or between the low tom and high tom:

 Exercise 1-178:

Do the same variations, but add the bass drum playing the "Charleston" rhythm:

 Exercise 1-179:

Exercise 1-180:

(When notating so many simultaneous parts in drums, there are some different ways to show the parts; notice the differences in notation style between the previous two exercises.)

Switch fluidly between these variations, for example, between playing the rhythm on snare and high tom, then on high tom and low tom:

Exercise 1-181:

Play quarter notes on ride cymbal, Charleston on snare drum, "two" and "four" on hi-hat, and the rhythm on bass drum:

Exercise 1-182:

Distribute the rhythm between limbs while playing accompanying parts — here is one example, but make up your own variations:

Exercise 1-183:

As I mentioned for pianists, you will soon get to know an exercise rhythm so well that it's time to move on to other rhythms. Do just a few of the variations with each exercise rhythm, but choose different variations each time in order to train yourself to be flexible.

Appendix V: Additional Sightreading

Finally, here is some additional sightreading with pitches you can do, regardless of the instrument you play (if you are a drummer, just read the rhythms). First, we'll play a series of exercises that are each thirty-two bars long. These can be performed unaccompanied, or over the chord progression known as "rhythm changes" found on pieces such as "Oleo," "Rhythm-a-ning," "I Got Rhythm," and many others. In this series of exercises, we start out with quarter note level rhythms, and progress to eighth note level, adding some triplets. All the exercises can be made more or less challenging based on the tempo at which you choose to read them. These are jazz-oriented with swing feel, but you can also find examples for reading practice from the vast literature of classical music and other musical styles.

This first exercise is entirely at the quarter note level:

Exercise 1-184:

In this exercise, we mix some quarter note and eighth note level passages:

Exercise 1-185:

Here, we have more eighth notes plus some triplets:

Exercise 1-186:

Finally, here is an exercise you can read with another person, each taking one part. If you don't have a colleague available for this, just read one individual part at a time yourself. I wrote it originally for guitarists, but you can adjust the octaves as necessary, depending on what range is comfortable for you on your instrument. Notice that the two parts are sometimes playing different rhythms, and sometimes playing the same rhythm together:

Exercise 1-187:

(this exercise continues on next page)

Another great source for sightreading is transcriptions of improvised solos. In *THE RHYTHM BOOK—Rhythmic Development and Performance in 4/4*, you will work on transcribing these yourself. For now, here are a couple examples.

Here is an exercise on a simple blues in F, inspired by the last chorus Wayne Shorter played in his improvised solo on "Eighty-One" from the Miles Davis recording *E.S.P.*

This exercise, which can be played over modal harmony found in pieces such as "So What" and "Impressions," is inspired by a Miles Davis solo from the classic recording *Kind of Blue*.

 (this exercise continues on next page)

About the Author

New York-based jazz guitarist and composer Rory Stuart has led critically acclaimed groups and played as a sideman with a number of major figures in the history of jazz. Described as "perhaps THE most innovative straight-ahead jazz guitarist to emerge in years," by *Jazz Times*, Rory has led the rhythm curriculum since 1992 at the world-renowned New School for Jazz and Contemporary Music. A list of his former students reads like a "Who's Who" of rising young jazz stars.

The recipient of Awards from the National Endowment for the Arts, Meet the Composer, and the Fulbright Commission, he has directed jazz workshops in Italy, Singapore, and Korea and performed and taught around the world, including in Argentina, Austria, the Bahamas, Brazil, Canada, Chile, Columbia, the Czech Republic, Denmark, Germany, Greece, Israel, Iceland, India, Israel, Italy, Kazakhstan, Korea, Poland, Portugal, Spain, Sweden, Switzerland, and the USA.

For more information, please see www.rorystuart.com.

About the Rhythm Book series:

THE RHYTHM BOOK — Beginning Notation and Sight-Reading:
• introduces rhythmic notation, from the very first steps (does not assume you have any notation background);
• teaches how to read and write rhythms in 4/4 at the quarter, eighth, and triplet eighth levels;
• creates a solid foundation on which further notation and sight-reading skills can be built.

THE RHYTHM BOOK — Intermediate Notation and Sight-Reading:
• builds from knowledge of quarter, eighth, and triplet eighths;
• progresses systematically from 16th notes through triplets of all rates, triple meters, odd meters, and even 32nd notes and beyond;
• prepares you to read and correctly write nearly any rhythms you will ordinarily encounter.

THE RHYTHM BOOK — Rhythmic Development and Performance in 4/4: Master rhythmic performance in 4/4. This volume:
• examines rhythmic styles and feels, including swing, Afro-Cuban, Brazilian, funk, calypso, reggae, and ballads;
• discusses phrasing, relationship to the beat, feeling time and form, defining the time in your playing, very fast and slow tempos, playing with others and rhythmically interacting, and how to develop rhythm ideas;
• includes numerous examples, as well as worksheets for suggested transcription projects.

THE RHYTHM BOOK — Crossrhythms on 4/4: Crossrhythms (aka implicit polymeter or groupings) are a powerful tool to expand your vocabulary in performance and composing. Perhaps the most under-represented rhythmic area in musical education, their study brings surprising benefits, including greater depth and freedom over harmonic forms. This volume:
• provides a systematic method for learning any crossrhythm;
• presents crossrhythms on 4/4 comprehensively, from most common/simple to rare/complex;
• incorporates many exercises and examples from different musical genres.

THE RHYTHM BOOK — Odd Meters and Changing Meters: Aimed at developing the reader's performance and composition skills with odd and changing meters, this volume:
• provides a systematic way to learn any new meter;
• explores odd meters in depth, different flavors of changing meters, and crossrhythms on odd meters;
• includes interesting examples from a wide variety of musical styles and exercises to develop your mastery.

THE RHYTHM BOOK — Superimposition and Subdivision, Metric Modulation, Feel Modulation and Displacement: With focus on some of the most challenging rhythmic areas in 21st Century music, this volume:
• offers systematic ways to learn rhythm superimpositions and convert between superimposition and subdivision;
• teaches a series of methods for performing metric modulations;
• presents exercises to address the challenges of feel modulation and feel displacement;
• demonstrates how to combine techniques (e.g. crossrhythms at superimposition rates over odd meters).

Train Your Ears

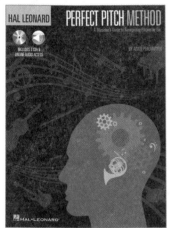

HAL LEONARD PERFECT PITCH METHOD
A Musician's Guide to Recognizing Pitches by Ear
by Adam Perlmutter

Perfect pitch is largely a misunderstood phenomenon. The *Hal Leonard Perfect Pitch Method* is designed to help you develop a sense of perfect pitch. In the process, your overall musicianship will benefit and you'll start listening to music on a deeper level and getting more satisfaction from it. At the heart of this book is a series of 49 ear-training sessions, one per day for seven weeks, using the included CDs or the online audio.
00311221 Book with 3 CDs and
Online Audio Access . $29.99

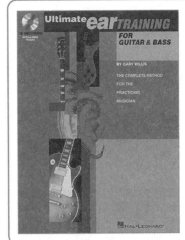

ULTIMATE EAR TRAINING FOR GUITAR AND BASS
by Gary Willis

Everything you need to improve your ear training, including a CD with 99 full-demo tracks, vital information on intervals, rhythms, melodic shapes, inversions, scales, chords, extensions, alterations, fretboard visualization, and fingering diagrams.
00695182 Book/CD Pack $17.99

BEGINNING EAR TRAINING
by Gilson Schachnik
Berklee Press

Introduces the core skills of ear training. Teaches how to: learn melodies by ear; sight-sing; internalize rhythms and melodies; improve pitch and timing; transpose; use solfege; transcribe and notate; and much more!
50449548 Book/Online Audio $16.99

ESSENTIAL EAR TRAINING FOR THE CONTEMPORARY MUSICIAN
by Steve Prosser
Berklee Press

The Ear Training curriculum of Berklee College of Music is known and respected throughout the world. Now, for the first time, this unique method has been captured in one comprehensive book by the chair of the Ear Training Department. This method teaches musicians to hear the music they are seeing, notate the music they have composed or arranged, develop their music vocabulary, and understand the music they are hearing. The book features a complete course with text and musical examples, and studies in rhythm, sight recognition, sol-fa, and melody.
50449421 .... $16.95

BERKLEE MUSIC THEORY – 2ND EDITION
by Paul Schmeling
Berklee Press

This essential method features rigorous, hands-on, "ears-on" practice exercises that help you explore the inner working of music, presenting notes, scales, and rhythms as they are heard in pop, jazz, and blues. You will learn and build upon the basic concepts of music theory with written exercises, listening examples, and ear training exercises. The online audio will help reinforce lessons as you begin to build a solid musical foundation. Now available with an answer key!
50449615 Book 1 .... $24.99
Also Available:
50449616 Book 2 .... $22.99

MUSIC THEORY
A Practical Guide for All Musicians
by Barrett Tagliarino

Get the rock-solid fundamentals of rhythm, pitch and harmony with this easy-to-use book/CD pack. Learn the universal language used by all musicians, regardless of instrument. Includes concise, detailed explanations, illustrations and written exercises with online audio examples and practice drills. This book will teach you how to: construct scales, chords and intervals; identify major and minor key centers and common chord progressions; accurately play various rhythm feels and figures; learn the basic principles of form and compositional analysis.
00311270 Book/Online Audio $15.99

Great Harmony & Theory Helpers

HAL LEONARD HARMONY & THEORY – PART 1: DIATONIC
by George Heussenstamm

This book is designed for anyone wishing to expand their knowledge of music theory, whether beginner or more advanced. The first two chapters deal with music fundamentals, and may be skipped by those with music reading experience. Topics include: basic music-reading instruction; triads in root position; triads in inversion; cadences; non-harmonic tones; the dominant seventh chord; other seventh chords; and more.
00312062..$27.50

HAL LEONARD HARMONY & THEORY – PART 2: CHROMATIC
by George Heussenstamm

Part 2 – Chromatic introduces readers to modulation and more advanced harmonies, covering: secondary dominants; borrowed chords; the Neapolitan 6th chord; augmented 6th chords; 9th, 11th, and 13th chords; and more. In addition to text, the book features many musical examples that illustrate the concepts, and exercises that allow readers to test and apply their knowledge.
00312064..$27.50

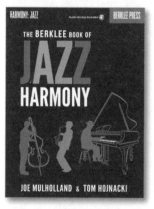

THE BERKLEE BOOK OF JAZZ HARMONY
by Joe Mulholland & Tom Hojnacki
Berklee Press

Learn jazz harmony, as taught at Berklee College of Music. This text provides a strong foundation in harmonic principles, supporting further study in jazz composition, arranging, and improvisation. It covers basic chord types and their tensions, with practical demonstrations of how they are used in characteristic jazz contexts; an accompanying recording lets you hear how they can be applied.
00113755 Book/Online Audio $27.50

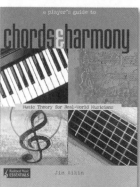

A PLAYER'S GUIDE TO CHORDS AND HARMONY
Music Theory for Real-World Musicians
by Jim Aikin
Backbeat Books

If you'd like to know about music theory but don't want to get bogged down in a stuffy college-level textbook, this guide was written just for you! Covers: intervals, scales, modes, triads and advanced voicings; interpreting chord symbols and reading sheet music; voice leading, chord progressions, and basic song forms; classical, jazz & pop; and more, with helpful quizzes and answers.
00331173..$19.95

ENCYCLOPEDIA OF READING RHYTHMS
Text and Workbook for All Instruments
by Gary Hess
Musicians Institute Press

A comprehensive guide to notes, rests, counting, subdividing, time signatures, triplets, ties, dotted notes and rests, cut time, compound time, swing, shuffle, rhythm studies, counting systems, road maps and more!
00695145 ....$19.95

THE CHORD WHEEL
The Ultimate Tool for All Musicians
by Jim Fleser

Master chord theory ... in minutes! *The Chord Wheel* is a revolutionary device that puts the most essential and practical applications of chord theory into your hands. This tool will help you: Improvise and Solo – Talk about chops! Comprehend key structure like never before; Transpose Keys – Instantly transpose any progression into each and every key; Compose Your Own Music – Watch your songwriting blossom! No music reading is necessary.
00695579 ....$14.99

MUSIC THEORY WORKBOOK
For All Musicians
by Chris Bowman

A self-study course with illustrations and examples for you to write and check your answers. Topics include: major and minor scales; modes and other scales; harmony; intervals; chord structure; chord progressions and substitutions; and more.
00101379 ....$12.99

THE ULTIMATE KEYBOARD CHORD CHART

This convenient reference features 120 of the most commonly used chords, easy diagrams, and information on chord theory.
00220016 ....$3.50

HAL•LEONARD®